PLANTS

Text by
David Squire

Illustrations by
Lisa Horstman

COLLINS
London and Glasgow

First published 1987
© in the text David Squire 1987
© in the illustrations Lisa Horstman 1987

ISBN 0 00 458867 3

Lisa Horstman wishes to express particular thanks to the Luton
Branch of the British Cactus and Succulent Society and especially
the late Mr R.E.Chinner.

Colour reproduction by Adroit Photo Litho, Birmingham
Filmset by Wordsmiths, London
Printed and bound by Wm Collins Sons and Co Ltd, Glasgow

10 9 8 7 6 5 4 3 2 1

Contents

Introduction

The range of houseplants is extensive, from some that have been tried and tested in homes for many decades to others that are newer introductions or have become easier to grow in lighter and brighter, glass-dominated, modern homes. Such homes are also often superbly insulated and enable high temperatures to be achieved economically, but whatever the temperature or brightness of your home, there are many plants to choose from.

In this book the plants are arranged taxonomically – following a system of plant classification according to their natural evolution and flower characteristics. Each plant is identified by its scientific name, also known as its botanical or Latin name, and includes both the genus and species. These are rather like surnames and christian names, but in reverse. A genus is formed of several species, while a group of related genera are classified together into a family.

Where a variety of a plant has arisen during its natural cultivation, this is indicated by placing single quotation marks around the name. For example, several coloured forms of the India Rubber Plant, *Ficus elastica*, have been raised in cultivation, and are called cultivars or cultivated varieties. Sometimes, distinctive forms of a particular plant develop naturally. These are called botanical varieties or sub-species and indicated by a further name being added to the genus and species names. Because botanists occasionally change their minds about the classification of a plant, earlier scientific names, known as synonyms, are also given – in brackets. Where a plant has a common name – or names – these are also given.

The country or area from which each plant originated is indicated. Some plants are hybrids, man-made by botanists and nurserymen, and do not have a native country. These are indicated by an x placed between a plant's first name (the genus) and the second (the species).

The expected height (shown as **H**) and spread (**S**) are given in both metric and imperial measurements – but remember that plants are living members of the home and may differ slightly. Climbers especially vary and adjust to the size and shape of the supporting framework they are given. The minimum desirable winter temperature, shown as **WT**, and the amount of light needed both in winter, **W**, and in summer, **S**, are indicated using these symbols:

☼	full sun	◎	indirect light
○	direct light without full sun	◉	light shade

Those plants that enjoy light shade will also tolerate heavy shade for short periods.

At the end of the description of each plant, the methods and times of propagation are indicated, whether from seeds, cuttings (stem, leaf-stem or leaf-cuttings), division, air-layering or runners.

Displaying plants indoors

Pots and containers Before the late 1950s, house-plants were invariably grown in earthenware clay pots that had a natural colour and texture. Then, plastic pots were introduced and the whole pot plant scene changed. Both square and round pots became available, in a range of colours. They are easily stored when not in use, their smooth surfaces are easily kept clean, and the plants in them require less moisture than those in clay pots. Plastic saucers, in which to stand pots, help in the watering of plants and keep surfaces beneath moisture free.

In addition to clay and plastic pots, many other containers are available. If they have base holes to allow excess water to escape plants can be planted directly into them, if not place a plastic or clay pot inside them. The Victorians and Edwardians created many specialized and distinctive containers, including ornate stands for palms and aspidistras and a wide variety of objects can be used as plant holders.

Wall-mounted plant holders, formed from wicker-work or plastic-covered wire, help to position trailing plants at eye-height, as well as creating a focal point along a wall. Suitable foliage plants include variegated ivies, Mother of Thousands *Saxifraga stolonifera*, Creeping Fig *Ficus pumila*, tradescantias, *Zebrina pendula* and the Devil's Ivy *Scindapsus aureus*. Flowering plants include *aeschyananthus* and *columnea*

8

species, as well as *Campanula isolphylla*, an ideal plant for cool but bright porches.

Indoor hanging-baskets, with built-in trays to prevent water dripping on floors and furniture, enable both foliage and flowering trailing plants to be positioned at eye-height. Hang one where heads cannot unexpectedly meet it, and make sure it is accessible when the compost needs to be watered. All trailing plants are suitable, including cascading ferns.

Plants trailing from the sides or corners of shelves can look just as exciting.

Plants in troughs Plastic troughs, depending on their length, are ideal for displaying three to six plants.

Troughs, about 15cm (6in) deep, allow pots to be stood in them, with damp peat packed between. This helps to create a humid atmosphere and decreases the amount of water needed. Troughs, especially when on legs, create room dividers. Use trailing plants to soften the trough's edges, and upright foliage plants to create height. By leaving plants in their pots seasonal changes can be easily made. Troughs can also be placed on window-sills, to obscure unpleasant views.

Large floor-level containers Large-leaved foliage plants can create a focal point, including many of the ficus family; if – with time – they become bare at their bases, place smaller plants around them.

Grouping plants Many plants benefit from being grouped together, creating a climate more humid than if they were on their own. Use several large foliage plants at the back, with low-growing foliage and flowering plants at the front. Place individual pots in a large, shallow, plastic tray, with an inch or so of clean shingle in its base, or stand each in a saucer. Remember that they all require different amounts of water.

'Bottle' gardens

The idea of growing plants in closed containers – so that water vapour, given off by the leaves, condenses on the glass and returns to the compost – was popularized in the early 1840s by Dr Nathaniel Ward, who, while trying to pupate a moth in a closed jar, discovered that plants could grow there.

Glass containers - carboys or large bottles - offer the best conditions. Avoid plastic, as moisture remains in clouds on its surface, obsuring the plants. On glass, it quickly condenses and runs into the compost.

When selecting plants for closed containers avoid invasive, large and fast growing plants, and those with soft, hairy leaves that would soon rot in a very humid atmosphere.

Small ferns, slow-growing palms like the Parlour Palm *Chamaedorea elegans*, small and smooth-leaved plants such as the Aluminium Plant *Pilea cadierei* 'Nana', Creeping Fig *Ficus pumila*, and small-leaved and variegated ivies are suitable. Low-growing cryptanthus (*Cryptanthus acaulis*, *C. bivittatus*, and *C. fosterianus*) are ideal; *Sansevieria hahnii*, young neoregalias and codiaeums and smooth-leaved peperomias can also be used. Remove plants that become too large or prune regularly to restrain their size.

Setting plants in carboys Thoroughly clean the container with soapy water, then use plenty of clean water to rinse it out. When dry, cover the base with 6.5cm/2½in of charcoal and pebbles (less for small containers). Use a funnel to add a thin layer of peat and sufficient loam-based compost to accommodate the depth of the roots. Sometimes, the neck of the bottle is wide enough to use your hands to set and firm the plants into position; if not, use a small hand-fork tied to a cane. Set large plants in position first, then smaller ones around them. Brush compost from the foliage and syringe the inside of the glass to remove compost. Then, put on the stopper.

It takes several hours for moisture to seep through the compost and for plants to give off water vapour. If moisture condenses on the inside of the glass and runs down into the compost, the right moisture content has been achieved. If not, repeat the spraying until the atmosphere is saturated with moisture.

Camouflaging and highlighting room features
Careful positioning of plants can highlight attractive windows, recesses and arches and hide unattractive

features. Large distinctively shaped plants take the eye away from them.

Climbing and trailing plants are ideal for screening pipes, but take care that the foliage does not touch hot-water pipes. Ivies, Grape Ivy *Rhoicissus rhomboidea*, Sweetheart Vine *Philodendron scandens* and Kangaroo Vine *Cissus antarctica* are climbers, while the Devil's Ivy *Scindapus aureus*, tradescantias and *Zebrina pendula* are suitable trailers.

Seasonal improvements to unsightly – but often essential – parts of the home, such as large radiators, are possible with the use of trailing types, as well as large, foliage plants set alongside them. Large troughs, packed with plants, can also be used.

Large arches, that otherwise might appear bare, look superb with a large, climbing plant clothing their edges. A supporting framework will be required.

Recesses, especially light coloured ones, look superb with a large foliage plant in them. Large palms, large-leaved ficus plants, *Brassaia actinophylla* and *Schefflera arboricola* are ideal. Alternatively, place a small trough of flowering houseplants at the base and use a hanging-basket to display the Bird's Nest Fern *Asplenium nidus* or a large *Nephrolepis* fern.

Illuminating plants

All natural or artifical light will highlight a plant, but only light within a certain wavelength will activate the green pigments in leaves and initiate growth. Ordinary light bulbs (tungsten-filament types) do not encourage growth. Indeed, if placed too close to plants their warmth increases the rate at which a plant breathes and gives off moisture, without helping with growth. They may also burn the foliage. In a small, partially enclosed position, use a 'cool' light from a flourescent tube.

Use spotlights to highlight plants in dull corners, especially during winter, and mirrors to give an impression of greater space.

Sunlight, plant growth-lights and some fluorescent tubes do initiate growth. If you do have special lights fitted, have then installed by a competent electrician.

The influence of light on flowering will vary from plant to plant. Some are termed short-day plants, initiating flowers buds when the length of darkness in every twenty-four hours is greater than the light part, some flower when the light period is longer than the dark part, and others do not have their flowering influenced by light or darkness. Nurserymen are able to control the length of darkness – and the temperature – and cause some plants, such as chrysanthemums and *Kalanchoe blossfeldiana* to flower at any time of the year.

Care and propagation

Part of the enjoyment of growing houseplants is growing more of them. The main methods of propagation are by seeds and by cuttings. Use the best seeds available, and always take cuttings from healthy parents.

Sowing seeds

Many flowering houseplants, such as cyclamen, cinerarias, calceolarias and primulas, can be raised from seeds. Suitable plants, and the time for sowing seeds, are indicated within the text. The basic needs for seeds to germinate are warmth, moisture and darkness, except for a few plants, such as primulas, which germinate better when exposed to light. Most seeds need a temperature of 16-18°C/61-64°F for rapid germination. In spring, this often can be provided on a warm sunny window-sill, with the sown pot of seeds covered with newspaper.

Sow seeds in small pots containing loam-based seed compost or a peat-based type. Place drainage crocks in the base and fill and firm the compost to 12mm/½in of the rim. Sow seeds thinly and evenly, covering them with fine compost to about three or four times their thickness. Stand the pot in 5cm/2in of water, until moisture rises to the surface. Place the pots in a box and cover with a pane of glass and sheet of newspaper. Turn the glass every day and wipe

15

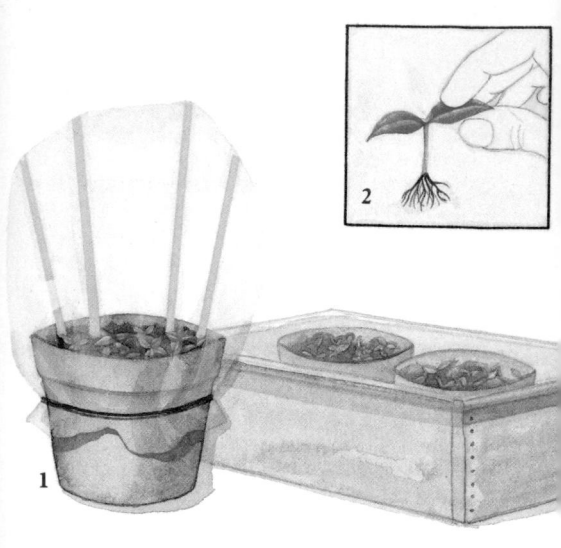

away the condensation. Remove both the glass and paper as soon as the seeds germinate. If just one pot has been sown, place it inside a plastic bag (**1**). As soon as the seedlings are growing strongly they can be lifted with a small plastic label and potted up. Hold the seedlings (**2**) by their seed leaves – the first to appear – as the stems are easily squashed.

Stem cuttings

These are formed from a healthy shoot, with a growing tip and a few inches of stem. Remove the lower leaves and trim the bases just below a leaf-joint (**3**). Insert and gently firm them 2.5-4cm/1-1½in into well-drained and aerated compost. Set the cuttings 12-18mm/½-¾in in from the side of the pot and place in a plastic bag, kept away from the cuttings by small canes (**4**). Position in good light, but out of direct sunlight, and remove the bag as soon as the cuttings root.

Leaf-stem cuttings

Plants such as *saintpaulias* and some *peperomias* can be increased by leaf-stem cuttings. Sever leaves from a

healthy parent, with a long piece of stem attached. Trim this to 4cm/1½in long (**1**) and insert and gently firm it 18-25mm/¾-1in deep in well-drained compost (**2**). Place the pot in a plastic bag, removing it as soon as roots form. Pot up the rooted cuttings singly into small pots (**3**).

Leaf cuttings

Increase large-leaved begonias by this method. Select a mature leaf, turn it upside down and with a sharp knife slit main and secondary veins (**4**). Place the leaf the right way up on compost in a box or large pot and peg it down with pieces of bent wire (**5**). Place the container in a plastic bag, removing it as soon as shoots develop. Pot them separately in small pots (**6**).

Runners

This is an easy way to increase plants, such as chlorophytums and *Saxifraga stolonifera*, that produce runners. With chlorophytums, place the mother plant in a box of compost and peg the tips of the runners

into the compost (**8**). Alternatively, with both chlorophytums and *Saxifraga stolonifera*, place small pots of compost around the parent and peg the runners into them (**7**). As soon as roots form, sever the plantlets and pot them separately.

Air layering

Rubber Plants *Ficus elastica*, cordylines and dracaenas that grow too high or reveal long, bare stems at their bases can be revitalized and decreased in height by encouraging the stem to develop roots. Below the lowest, healthy leaf, make a sloping upward cut, about two-thirds through the stem (**1**). Wedge it open with a match-stick. Tie a piece of polythene around the stem, 5-6.5cm/2-2½in below the cut, and pack moist peat around it (**2**). Then, secure the polythene around the top. When roots can be seen through the

polythene (**3**), sever the stem below the roots (**4**) and pot up into a large pot. Initially, it may be necessary to support the plant with a cane. If the lower part is kept, it may eventually develop shoots from old leaf-joints.

Watering houseplants

More plants are killed each year through being excessively watered than for any other reason. Growing a plant in artificial conditions, where it may have an extensive array of foliage but a relatively small amount of compost for its roots, demands a skill not easily learned. For most plants, the compost should be slightly moist at all times, which nurserymen achieve with capillary watering systems, but with only a watering-can, the moisture in the compost is bound to fluctuate between being over and under moist.

The porous nature of clay pots enables air and moisture to pass through. Plastic pots, with their smooth, non-porous sides, retain moisture and need less watering. Because they do not have the cooling effect of water passing through their sides, the compost in plastic pots is usually warmer than if in a clay pot. This is an advantage during winter, but a disadvantage during summer.

Judging when a plant needs water

- If the pot is made of clay, it can be tapped with a cotton-reel spiked on a short bamboo cane.

If the sound is dull, water is not needed, if the note rings, then a thorough soaking is essential.

- If the compost's surface is light coloured, it often indicates the need for water, but beware that compost lower down may be too wet.
- Lifting the pot and plant and judging its weight is another method, but it does need experience – and a small plant. As the compost dries it weighs less.
- The appearance of the plant is usually a good guide, although many will also wilt if the compost is kept continually wet, causing the roots to die. If the compost does become too wet, remove the plant from the pot and leave the soil-ball exposed until the plant recovers. Take care that the soil-ball does not crumble, as the roots may then dry out and become damaged.

How to water

- The best method is to stand the pot in a bowl containing water 5-7cm/2-3in deep, until moisture percolates to the surface. Then remove the pot and allow excess water to drain.
- If the plant is standing in a saucer, fill the saucer with water. Empty the saucer when moisture appears on the surface of the compost.

- If the plant is too large to move and is standing in a large saucer, water the compost through a small watering-can. Many small plants can also be watered by this method, but take care not to splash moisture on the foliage or flowers, especially during winter.

- Capillary watering systems are available, where a plant is stood directly on a bed of sand or fine shingle, automatically kept moist at all times. Moisture passes into the compost by capillary action. Do not allow the sand or shingle to become dry. If this happens, roots penetrating the bed will soon die.

- Urn Plants and many other bromeliads, which form a funnel of leaves at their tops, can be additionally watered by keeping the urn filled up with water.

Repotting houseplants

Many plants live quite happily in small pots for a long time, but others need repotting into larger ones as soon as the compost is full of roots, often annually. This is indicated when roots emerge from the drainage hole at the base of the pot and a thick layer forms around the soil-ball. Loam-type composts, based on John Innes formulations, or the newer peat-based types can be used. Peat-based types are especially suited to small plants, such as saintpaulias and peperomias, while the heavier loam-based ones are better for larger plants, where they create a much more secure base.

When repotting a plant first, remove the pot, supporting the soil-ball (**1**). If the pot does not come easily away from the soil-ball, knock the edge of the

container on a firm surface. Place the plant in a slightly larger clean pot, with broken crocks in its base covered with a layer of peat (**2**). Trickle compost around the soil-ball (**3**), and gently firm it with your fingers to within 12-18mm/½-¾in of the rim. Lastly, gently water the compost, without too much disturbance (**4**).

Feeding houseplants

Throughout late spring and summer, most houseplants need regular feeding, either from concentrated liquid feeds, special pellets or sticks that slowly release plant foods into the compost. Follow the maker's instructions precisely.

Grooming plants

Houseplants often become dusty. Those with large, smooth leaves can be cleaned by using a soft damp duster or sponge to wash them. Use a dry cloth to remove all moisture, which acts as a lens when under strong summer sunlight. Proprietary leaf-cleaning solutions are available. Use a soft brush to dust plants with hairy leaves.

Houseplants in winter

Houseplants are more difficult to look after in winter than during summer, when there is plenty of light and they are growing strongly. If plants are given too much water during winter, when they cannot use it, the compost becomes excessively wet for long periods. If the temperature is too high, when the amount and duration of light is low, a spindly, straggly and sickly plant will result.

In winter remember:

- Do **not** splash water on the foliage or around the bases of plants – it encourages diseases.
- Do **not** keep the compost continually saturated. However, plants in flower should not be deprived of moisture.
- Do **not** feed plants during winter, as they will not be able to use the extra nutrients when the light is poor and they are not growing strongly.
- Do **not** place plants in draughts or fluctuating temperatures, especially when in flower.
- Do **not** leave diseased stems or leaves on plants, as they will soon cause other parts to rot. Soft-leaved plants, and those in flower, are especially susceptible to rotting.
- Do **not** place plants on top of hot radiators. The compost soon dries – and even bakes if too hot.
- Do **not** leave plants on window-sills overnight during cold spells.
- Do **not** trap plants between curtains and a window, as here the temperature falls quickly.
- Do **not** keep the compost too wet. Many plants can be safely given low temperatures during winter, if the compost is kept slightly dry.

Holiday care for houseplants

Caring for treasured houseplants all year and then leaving them untended when on holiday can lead to disaster. But it need not happen. Even if no one is available to look after them, there are a number of simple measures you can take yourself.

- Stand the plants on the floor in a cool, north- or east-facing room.
- Stand the pots in 10-15cm/4-6in deep plastic trays and pack moist peat around them.
- Stand the pots in plastic trays, shallowly filled with water.
- Insert wicks into the compost at the tops of pots and trail the other ends up into a pot of water.

POLYPODY FAMILY **Stagshorn Fern** *Platycerium bifurcatum* (= *P. alicorne*) (**1**) is a distinctive evergreen Australian fern that uses trees for support, growing in crevices and joints full of moist and decaying leaves which provide its nutrients. It is superb when grown attached to a piece of wood wrapped in sphagnum moss and suspended from a wall or shelf, rather like a hanging-basket. Keep the compost moist and ensure water does not splash on the antler-like fronds. H:45-75cm/1½-2½ft; S:45-75cm/1½-2½ft; WT:10-13°C/50-55°F; W:◉; S:◎/◉; spores, early spring; division, spring. *P. grande* is similar, but larger at 1.5-1.8m/5-6ft wide.

BUTTON FERN FAMILY **Button Fern** *Pellaea rotundifolia* (**3**), from New Zealand, is also known as the Cliff Brake Fern. It is distinctive and bushy, with small, rounded leaves borne on wiry stems, ideal for placing in a wall bracket, on a pedestal or in a small hanging-basket. Take care not to allow the compost to dry out. H:20cm/8in; S:25-38cm/10-15in; WT:10-13°C/50-55°F; W:○; S:◉; spores, early-spring; division, spring.

BRAKE FERN FAMILY **Ribbon Fern** *Pteris cretica* (**2**) is native to a wide area, from south-west Europe to Japan. Its short, rhizomatous rootstock develops narrow fronds. Always keep the compost moist. H:30-45cm/1-1½ft; S:23-38cm/9-15in; WT:7°C/45°F; W:○; S:◉-◑; spores, early spring; division, spring.

BRAKE FERN FAMILY (contd) ***Pteris ensiformis*** *(= P. crenata)* (**4**), from the Himalayas, and Ceylon to Australia, with its slender, deep green evergreen fronds, is quite similar to *P. cretica*, but is mostly seen in the outstandingly attractive form 'Victoriae'. This has smaller fronds, variegated white, forming an ideal plant for planting in a carboy or large, glass bottle. H:30-38cm/12-15in; S:25-30cm/10-12in; WT:13-16°C/55-61°F; W:○; S:◐-●; spores, early spring; division, spring.

Silver Brake Fern *Pteris quadriaurita argyraea (= P. biaurita argyraea/P. argyraea)* (**3**), from the tropics, is a superb and easily-grown fern, with long and tapering fronds, beautifully coloured and delicately lobed. It is ideal for a low table in a shaded alcove, where the fronds exhibit their best colour. H:30-60cm/1-2ft; S:25-60cm/10-30in; WT:10°C/50°F; W:○; S:◐-●; spores, early spring; division, spring. WT:7°C/45°F; W:◐; S:◐-●; spores, early spring; bulbils, spring to early summer; division, spring.

MAIDENHAIR FERN FAMILY **Maidenhair Fern** *Adiantum capillus-veneris* (**2**), from both sub-tropical and temperate zones, has such a wispy and delicate appearance that it belies the plant's resilience. Outdoors the triangular fronds die down during winter; indoors it is evergreen, warmth and humidity are then the key to success. H:15-25cm/6-10in; S:15-30cm/6-12in; WT:7°C/45°F; W:◐; S:◐-●; spores, early spring; division, spring.

Adiantum raddianum *(= A. cuneatum)* (**1**), from Brazil, is especially attractive when grown in an indoor hanging-basket, where its purple-black stems splay out and reveal the graceful and elegant evergreen triangular fronds. H:30-45cm/1-1½ft; S:45-60cm/1½-2ft; WT:7°C/45°F; W:◎; S:◎-◉; spores, early spring; division, spring.

1

2

Asplenium Fern Family **Asplenium bulbiferum** (**2**) is an easily recognizable Australian, New Zealand and Indonesian fern. The ease and novelty of the manner in which new plants can be raised increases its interest, especially for young children. The finely-cut, carrot-like fronds bear small bulbils (bulb-shaped growths) on their upper surfaces, which can be encouraged to form roots by placing an entire leaf on a box of peat-based compost. Use small pieces of wire to peg down the frond. Roots develop from the bases of the bulbils, when they can be potted individually. H:45-60cm/1½-2ft; S:60-90cm/2-3ft; WT:7°C/45°F; W:◎; S:◎-◉; spores, early spring; bulbils, spring to early summer; division, spring.

Bird's-nest Fern *Asplenium nidus* (= *A. nidus-avis*) is (**1**), to many eyes, the most distinctive and beautiful of all ferns. The large, spoon shaped, glossy leaves arise from a central base, like feathers on a shuttle-cock. On its tropical Asian and Pacific Island homes it anchors itself to trees but does not take food or moisture from its host. In the home it is best grown in a pot. Its symmetrical outline makes it ideal as a centre-piece for a dining table when not in use, and is also very attractive on a low table beneath a standard lamp. On Mauritius and other African islands, where there has been a French influence, it is known as *Langue de Boeuf*, Tongue of Beef, and its leathery fronds may reach 0.6-1.2m/2-4ft long and 20cm/8in wide.H:0.6-1m/2-3½ft; S:30-60cm/1-2ft; WT:13°C/55°F; W:◎; S:◎-◉; spores, early spring.

ASPLENIUM FERN FAMILY (contd) **Hart's Tongue Fern** *Phyllitis scolopendrium (= Scolopendrium vulgare)* (**2**) is a highly successful fern, growing throughout the northern hemisphere. Indoors, grow the beautifully-leaved forms, such as 'Crispum' with wavy and crested edges and the dwarf 'Cristatum' with crested tips. Its undemanding natures makes it suitable for shaded and cool places, especially during winter. Its wide native area has encouraged many common names, even within the British Isles. In Dorsetshire it has been known as Horse-tongue, in Somerset as Lamb's-tongue, in Hampshire as Longleaf, in parts of Ireland as Burntweed (from its use as a remedy for burns), in Guernsey as Christ's Hair and in North America as Deer's Tongue. H:30-60cm/1-2ft; S:30-50cm/12-20in; WT: 2°C/35°F; W:◎; S:◎-◉; spores, early spring ('Crispum' is sterile and can only be increased by vegetative methods).

HOLLY FERN FAMILY **Japanese Holly Fern** *Cyrtomium falcatum (= Polystichum falcatum)* (**1**), from China, Japan and the Himalayas, is ideal for the home. Its stiff, sickle-like leaflets are able to withstand adverse conditions experienced in many rooms during winter. The form 'Rochfordianum' at 30-45cm/1-1½ft high has wide displays of fronds with larger leaflets, wavy edged and revealing pointed tops. It is ideal for growing in cold bedrooms during winter, or for placing in a cool stairway, hall or landing. H:30-60cm/1-2ft; S:30-60cm/1-2ft; WT:7-10°C/45-50°F; W:◎; S:◉; division, spring.

1

2

1

2

SWORD FERN FAMILY **Sword Fern** or **Fishbone Fern** *Nephrolepis exaltata* (**2**), from the Tropics, displays the well-known fern-like type fronds arising from a central base. However, it is the many beautiful forms that are chiefly grown. 'Bostoniensis', the Boston Fern, displays cascading and tapering fronds up to 90cm/3ft long; 'Hillii' is superb when planted in an indoor hanging-basket or placed to cascade from a high shelf; 'Marshallii' develops densely crested fronds and is ideal in a large pot where the semi-upright fronds can be seen from above; 'Elegantissima' is compact with closely overlapping fronds. Large and mature plants grown on pedestals are always eye-catching, with fronds cascading from all sides. H:45-75cm/1½-2½ft; S:0.75-1m/2½-3½ft; WT:10°C/50°F; W:◎; S:◎-◑; offset plantlets, spring to summer.

RABBIT'S-FOOT FERN FAMILY **Hare's-foot Fern** *Davallia canariensis* (**1**), from Spain, the Canary Islands and North Africa, is also known as Rabbit's-foot Fern and Squirrel's-foot Fern. It gains its names from the creeping, pale brown roots that resemble the feet of these animals. It grows best in an indoor hanging-basket, full of peat and sphagnum moss. It is ideal for growing in a kitchen, near a window and suspended over a sink. The creeping rhizomatous roots should be left exposed. Do not let the compost dry out. H:30-45cm/1-1½ft; S:45-60cm/1½-2ft; WT:10°C/50°F; W:○; S:◎; spores, early spring; division, spring.

FIG FAMILY This mainly Asian family of evergreen or deciduous shrubs and trees provides several well-known house-plants grown for their attractive foliage. In their native countries many achieve massive proportions, but when young are ideal for growing in pots indoors, a greenhouse or conservatory.

Increasing Ficus plants:: Take cuttings from mid-spring to early summer and insert them in equal parts peat and sharp sand. The cuttings of *Ficus benjamina*, *F. deltoidea*, *F. pumila* and *F. sagittata* 'Variegata' should be 5-10cm/2-4in long and rooted at 16°C/61°F. Those of *F. elastica* and *F. lyrata* should be 10-13cm/4-5in and rooted at 21°C/70°F.

Weeping Fig or **Benjamin Fig Tree** *Ficus benjamina* (= *F. nitida*) (**1**), also known as the Weeping Laurel and Small-leaved Rubber Plant, is a graceful, shade-loving tree-like plant from Asia. Its slightly pendulous branches bear stiff leaves, soft green at first, darkening later. It is ideal for setting in a large, bare corner, as its branches splay outwards and create a dominant feature. It is also called the Java Fig or Java Willow and is used as a street tree in Egypt. H:1.2-1.8m/4-6ft; S:0.9-1.2m/3-4ft; WT:13-16°C/55-61°F; W:○; S:○-◉; cuttings, spring to mid-summer; air-layering, early to mid-summer.

Mistletoe Fig *Ficus deltoidea* (= *F. diversifolia*) (**2**), from India and Malaysia, is also known as the Mistletoe Rubber Plant. It is slow growing, and displays leathery leaves. It gains its name from the

12mm/½in wide, long-stemmed, yellow or dull red berries borne throughout the year. It is ideal for a floor-standing pot, perhaps positioned at the back of flowering plants. H:30-75cm/1-2½ft; S:30-60cm/1-2ft; WT:7-10°C/45-50°F; W:○-◐; S:◐-●; cuttings, spring to mid-summer.

Indian Rubber Plant or **Rubber Plant** *Ficus elastica* (**1**), also known as Assam-rubber or Rambong-rubber, is a tropical Asian tree and an early source of rubber, originally used for erasers. It is ideal for standing at the side of a patio door, where it softens the window's outline and benefits from the good light. It is an ideal plant for offices, and later, when assuming a tree-like stance, it is ideal for foyers. When young, it displays an unbranched stem bearing stiff, glossy leaves, and is most frequently seen in the form 'Decora' with dark green leaves up to 30cm/1ft long. Others include 'Doescheri' (pink-tinted pale green leaves with ivory edges), 'Schryveriana' (variegated cream patches) and 'Tricolor' (cream variegations, often flushed pink). H:1.2-1.8m/4-6ft; S:45-60cm/1½-2ft; WT:16-18°C/61-64°F; W:○; S:○-◐; cuttings, spring to mid-summer; air-layering, early to mid-summer.

Fiddle-back Fig *Ficus lyrata* (= *F. pandurata*) (**2**), from West Africa, eventually achieves tree-like proportions, with distinctively shaped green leaves, often flushed golden-yellow. In the home it is best grown in a large, floor-standing pot near a window.

1　2

1

H:0.6-1.2m/2-4ft; S:30-60cm/1-2ft; WT:16-18°C/61-64°F; W:○; S:○-◉; cuttings, spring to mid-summer; air-layering, early to mid-summer.

FIG FAMILY (contd) **Creeping Fig** *Ficus pumila (= F. repens)* (**1**), from China, is also known as the Climbing Fig and Climbing Rubber Plant. It performs well as a climber or trailer. It is ideal for trailing from a shelf or indoor hanging-basket, and grows well in shady corners. The large, leathery adult leaves are rarely seen on pot plants, usually only present on those over

3.5m/12ft and grown in conservatories. H:45-60cm/
1½-2ft; S:15-23cm/6-9in; WT:7-10°C/45-50°F;
W:○-◉; S:◉-◉; cuttings, spring to mid-summer.

Trailing Fig *Ficus sagittata* 'Variegata' (= *F. radicans*) (**2**), from the East Indies, is a superb variegated plant, ideal for indoor hanging-baskets, pots in wall-brackets or even just trailing to soften the edge of a shelf, where it freely trails. It is useful for shaded corners that would benefit from the light colours of a variegated plant. H:7.5-10cm/3-4in; Trailing; WT:13-16°C/55-61°F; W:○-◉; S:◉-◉; cuttings, spring to mid-summer.

2

NETTLE FAMILY **Aluminium Plant** *Pilea cadierei* (**2**), from North Vietnam, was not initially thought to be of any worth as a houseplant and considered by a prominent botanist of the time to be an insignificant weed! Now it is well-known as an attractive foliage plant for the home, ideal for low tables, where the leaves can be admired from above. The silvery patterned leaves give rise to its common name. The normal species tends to become leggy and bare at its base and therefore it is usually grown in the home in the 23cm/9in high form 'Nana'. H:25-30cm/10-12in; S:30-38cm/12-15in; WT:10-13°C/50-55°F; W:○-◎; S:◎-◉; cuttings, early summer.

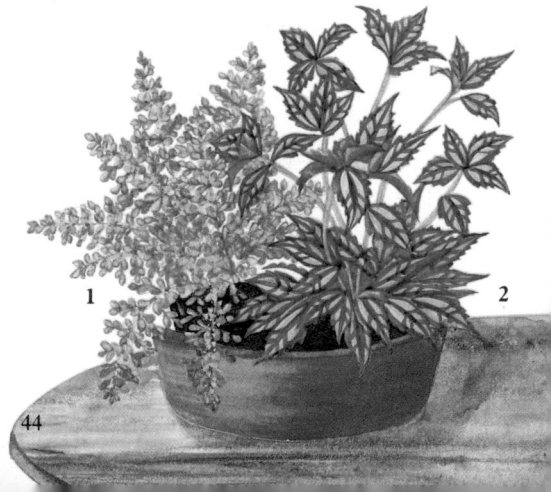

Artillery Plant or **Gunpowder Plant** *Pilea microphylla* (= *P. muscova*) (**1**), from Tropical America, found fame as a houseplant earlier than the Aluminium Plant. From early summer to autumn, pollen is puffed from anthers in the inconspicuous yellow-green flowers, causing amusement and interest. Children usually like to have this plant in the home. The whole plant is fern-like, bushy and densely-branched, and it grows well in shady corners - even dark and steamy bathrooms. H:20-25cm/8-10in; S:25-30cm/10-12in; WT:10-13°C/50-55°F; W:○-◉; S:◉-◑; cuttings, early summer.

Baby's Tears or **Mind Your Own Business** *Soleirolia soleirolii* (= *Helxine soleirolii*) (**3**) has been described as a delicate little weed from Corsica with minute green flowers and prostrate pale to mid green leaves. However, there are also many forms with beautifully coloured or variegated leaves. These include 'Argentea' with silver variegations and 'Aurea' displaying golden-green leaves. The stems root and eventually the plant forms an attractive mat of leaves; sometimes becoming invasive. It is ideal for creating an attractive

3

1

backcloth for other plants, especially during winter. Prostrate and spreading; WT:4-7°C/39-45°F; W:○-◎; S:◎-●; division, spring to mid-summer.

PROTEA FAMILY **Silky Oak** or **Silk Oak** *Grevillea robusta* (**1**) comes from Southern Australia, where its tree-like stature yields prettily marked wood prized by furniture makers. In Sri Lanka it has been used for shade in tea plantations, as a windbreak and as fuel. In homes and cool greenhouses its silky hair-covered fern-like leaves create interest the entire year. It is superb as a large, floor-standing plant, with small plants set around it. Neutral or slightly acid soil is essential. During summer, place your *Grevillea* outdoors on a sheltered patio. H:0.9-1.8m/3-6ft; S:38-50cm/15-20in; WT:4-7°C/39-45°F; W·☼-◐; S:○-◎; seeds early spring

BOUGAINVILLEA FAMILY ***Bougainvillea* x *buttiana*** (**2**) is an exceptionally beautiful summer to autumn flowering climber for a large pot in the home or conservatory. Earlier this century it was found in a Columbian priest's garden by Mrs R. V. Butt, and is now widely grown. The insignificant flowers are surrounded by very large crimson to magenta bracts, which are modified leaves. In pots it can be restrained to 1.5-2.1m/5-7ft high, and will need canes for support. It is ideal for brightening up the surround of a large window, and trailing over a patio window. WT:7°C/45°F; W:☼; S:☼-○; cuttings, mid-summer.

BOUGAINVILLEA FAMILY (contd) **Paper Flower**
Bougainvillea glabra (**3**), from Brazil, is the best
species for room cultivation as it flowers when still
quite small. From late summer to early autumn it
displays 15-23cm/6-9in long clusters of insignificant
white flowers surrounded by bracts in shades of red
and purple. Young plants can be kept bushy and
compact by snipping off the tips of stems when
15cm/6in long, and even in a large pot it can be
restrained to 1.2-1.5m/4-5ft high. Its best grown in a
floor-standing pot, placed near a large window. Use
canes and wires to support the plant. WT:7°/45°F;
W:☼; S:☼-○; cuttings, mid-summer.

PEBBLE PLANT FAMILY *Conophytum biliobum* (=
Derenbergia biloba) (**2**), from South and South-west
Africa, is an easily recognisable diminutive succulent,
ideal for a window-sill. It is ideal for a sunny kitchen.
The two-lobed body is grey at first, slowly becoming
red and as the plant ages several grow together to
form a small cluster. The 12mm/½in wide yellow
flowers appear during late summer and early autumn.
H:4-5cm/1½-2in; S:18-25mm/¾-1in but spreading
to form a clump; WT:5°C/41°F; W:☼; S:☼-○;
seeds, early summer; division, summer.

Conophytum frutescens (= *C. salmonicolor*) (**1**), from
South and South-west Africa, is another clump-
forming succulent, with a divided, heart-shaped,
green body and 12mm/½in wide orange-pink
flowers from mid to late summer. With age, the plant

48

sometimes develops stems up to 13cm/5in high, but is usually seen in its small form. Any sunny window ledge suits it, even a kitchen or bathroom. H:2.5cm/1in; S:12mm/½in but spreading to form a clump; WT:5°C/41°F; W:☼; S:☼-○; seeds, early summer; division, summer.

PEBBLE PLANT FAMILY (cont) **Tiger's Jaws** *Faucaria tigrina* (**1**), from Cape Province, is an ideal succulent for a sunny window-sill. It is formed of short stems bearing four to five pairs of colourful, teeth-edged leaves, giving rise to its common name. Eventually it forms a cluster, with 5cm/2in wide, golden-yellow, daisy-like flowers during late summer and early autumn. The flowers open during sunny afternoons, closing at night. H:5-6.5cm/2-2½in; S:10-13cm/4-5in; WT:5°C/41°F; W:☼; S:☼-○; seeds, spring; cuttings, mid to late summer.

Lithops bella (**2**), from South-west Africa, belongs to a group of succulents collectively known as Pebble Plants or Living Stones, names acquired from their resemblance to pebbles. The pale grey, pebble-like body, with dark markings at the top, is formed of a

50

pair of thickened and swollen leaves joined at their base. Daisy-like flowers appear from between the leaves during early autumn. Eventually it spreads to form a clump. Successful on a warm, sunny window-sill, try growing it in a collection of succulents on a kitchen window. H:2.5cm/1in; S:2.5-4cm/1-1½in and spreading; WT:5°C/41°F; W:☼; S:☼-◐; seeds, mid-spring; division, mid-summer.

Lithops optica, from Namaqualand, develops a grey-green body with a deep cleft between the two fused leaves that form the plant. It eventually creates a clump. White daisy-like flowers appear during mid-winter. The form *L. o. rubra* (**3**) displays a very attractive purple-red body, and is more readily available than the species. H:18mm/¾in; S:2.5-

51

3cm/1-1¼in; WT:5°C/41°F; W:☼; S:☼-○; seeds, mid-spring; division, mid-summer.

AMARANTH FAMILY **Celosia argentea** *(not illustrated)*, from Tropical Asia, is a bright annual for summer colour indoor or in a greenhouse. It displays 7.5cm/3in wide, silvery-white, feather-like plumes from mid-summer to autumn. It is not difficult to grow and is frequently seen in the following two superb forms.

Cockscomb *Celosia argentea cristata* (**1**) is a mid-summer to autumn fascination with its 7.5-13cm/3-5in wide densely crested heads of red, orange or yellow flowers. H:30cm/1ft; S:20-25cm/8-10in; WT:18°C/64°F for seed sowing; W:☼; S:☼; seeds, late winter.

Prince of Wales Feather *Celosia argentea plumosa* *(= C. a. pyramidalis)* (**2**) creates brightly coloured 7.5-15cm/3-6in high, pyramidal and feathery, spires in colours including pink, yellow, crimson and amber from mid to late summer. The Lilliput strains at 30cm/1ft high are best for growing indoors in pots. It is ideal for cool but bright rooms during summer, such as bedrooms. Do not confuse this plant with the similarly named Prince's Feather or Pygmy Torch *Amaranthus hypochondriacus*, a half-hardy annual widely used in summer-bedding displays. H:30-60cm/1-2ft; S:25-38cm/10-15in; WT:18°C/64°F for seed sowing; W:☼; S:☼; seeds, late winter.

CACTUS FAMILY The terms cactus and succulent are frequently used erroneously. All cacti are succulents, but not all succulents are cacti. Cacti belong to the Cactaceae family, which is just one of the several families that provide plants called succulents.

Cacti have leafless stems swollen with water-storage tissue that makes them the camels of the plant world. Many succulent plant enthusiasts consider cacti to the elite of the group and talk of cacti and other succulents. Cacti are distinguished from other succulents in having woolly or hairy tufts called aeroles. Botanically these are modified sideshoots unique to members of the Cactaceae family. All are superb on a sunny window-sill.

Rat's Tail Cactus *Aporocactus flagelliformis (= Cereus flagelliformis)* (**1**), from Mexico and formerly called Creeping Cereus, is an eye-catching plant, superb where the stems trail freely. From mid-spring to early summer it displays 7.5cm/3in long, funnel-shaped, magenta flowers along the 12mm/½in wide pendent stems. Eventually, these trail to 90cm/3ft. Rich, well-drained compost and a small indoor hanging-basket or 13cm/5in wide pot secured against a wall assure success. It is also suitable for placing on the corners of high, sunny shelves. Repot the plant annually, after the flowers fade. Trailing; S:20-38cm/8-15in; WT:5°C/45°F; W:☼; S:☼; seeds, early spring; cuttings, mid-spring to mid-summer.

Sand Dollar, **Silver Dollar** or **Star Cactus** *Astro-phytum asterias* (**2**), from Mexico, gains a further

name, Sea Urchin, from the unusual markings on its body. From mid to late summer this easily-grown cactus is crowned with 3cm/1¼in wide, sweetly-scented, red-throated, yellow flowers. H:3cm/1¼in; S:7.5cm/3in; WT:5-7°C/41-45°F; W:☼; S:☼; seeds, early spring.

1

2

3

CACTUS FAMILY (contd) **Goat's Horn Cactus** *Astrophytum capricorne* (**3**), from Mexico, is spectacular, with its ribbed body and curved, upward-pointing, flattened spines that appear from the upper half, like a goat's beard. These are surmounted, from mid to late summer, by 5cm/2in wide, red-centred, yellow flowers. H:20-25cm/8-10in; S:7.5-13cm/3-5in; WT:5-7°C/41-45°F; W:☼; S:☼; seeds, early spring.

Bishop's Cap Cactus *Astrophytum myriostigma* (**2**), from Mexico, is probably the most attractive member of this genus. The five- or six-ribbed grey body, initially globular then cylindrical, is blanketed with white scales. From mid to late summer it develops 4cm/1½in wide flowers in short tufts. This plant is often confused with the Bishop's Mitre Cactus *A. m. quadricostatum* which, although similar, has only four ribs running up its body. H:15-20cm/6-8in; S:10-15cm/4-6in; WT:5-7°C/41-45°F; W:☼; S:☼; seeds, early spring.

Old Man Cactus *Cephalocereus senilis* (= *Cephalophorus senilis*/*Pilocereus senilis*) (**1**) is well known in Mexico where aged plants up to 200 years old create columns rising to 12m/40ft high and 38-45cm/15-18in wide. In the home it is more manageable, with the pale green body displaying yellow spines and long white hairs that give rise to the common name. It seldom develops its white flowers until 4.5-6m/15-20ft high, so these are rarely seen in cultivation. H:20-60cm/8-24in; S:5-7.5cm/2-3in; WT:5-7.5°C/41-45°F; W:☼; S:☼; cuttings, late spring.

CACTUS FAMILY (contd) *Cereus peruvianus* (**1**), from Brazil and Argentina, is a widely grown representative of this genus, and creates a distinctive blue-green column. The ribs display stout spines. In the wild, it reaches 9m/30ft, but in a pot is restrained to an acceptable size for a home. The white flowers appear at night. H:60-90cm/2-3ft; S:7.5-13cm/3-5in; WT:5°C/41°F; W:☼; S:☼; seeds, mid-spring; cuttings, spring to mid-summer.

Silver Torch *Cleistocactus strausii* (= *Cereus strausii/ Pilocereus strausii*) (**2**) is a native of the Argentine and Bolivia, with the stance, but in miniature, of the tall, columnar cacti so often part of old Western movie scenes. It eventually forms large clusters of shallowly ribbed, slow-growing, upright stems, 5-7.5cm/2-3in wide. Only occasionally does it develop 7.5cm/3in long, tubular, scarlet flowers during mid to late summer, and even then they often only partly open. It is at its best as part of a landscaped desert scene in a conservatory, although in the home it creates a superb feature by the side of a patio window. H:0.9-1.8m/3-6ft; clump-forming; WT:5°C/41°F; W:☼; S:☼; seeds, early spring; cuttings, mid to late summer.

CACTUS FAMILY (contd) **Golden Barrel Cactus**
Echinocactus grusonii (**1**), from Central Mexico, lives
up to a literal translation of its first name: hedgehog-
like and prickly. Its large body, 90cm/3ft wide in the
wild, can resemble a rolled-up hedgehog, while the
spines afford formidable protection. So tough are
these spines that Mexicans have used them as
tooth-picks. In the home, on a sunny window-sill, the
plant is slow growing and seldom reaches more than
15cm/6in wide. During early summer old plants bear
5cm/2in wide, yellow flowers in a circle at their tops.
It is needs plenty of light. H:15cm/6in; S:15cm/6in;
WT:5-7°C/41-45°F; W:☼; S:☼; seeds, mid-spring.

Echinocereus knippelianus (**2**), from Central Mexico, usually spreads to form a 13-15cm/5-6in wide
clump of 5cm/2in wide stems. The wrinkled skin of
this rib-stemmed plant creates part of its attraction,

60

while in late spring and early summer 6.5cm/2½in wide flowers are another feature. H:7.5cm/3in; S:15cm/6in; WT:5°C/41°F; W:☼; S:☼; seeds, early spring; cuttings, spring to late summer.

Echinocereus pectinatus (**3**) is well-known in its native Mexico, where it is called Cabeza del Viego (Old Man's Cap). Its purplish, gooseberry-flavoured, fruits are eaten by Mexicans, and the flesh of the stems used as a vegetable - after the spines have been removed! During early summer it produces 7.5cm/ 3in long, bell-like, cerise-pink flowers. It is cylindrical and slow-growing, and old plants tend to branch. Take care not to water it excessively. H:20cm/8in; S:7.5cm/3in, but branching and spreading; WT:5°C/ 41°F; W:☼; S:☼; seeds, early spring; cuttings, spring to late summer.

3

1

2

CACTUS FAMILY (contd) **Echinopsis** Paramount Hybrid 'Peach Monarch' (**1**) is a beautiful desert cacti. During early summer, it reveals up to twelve, long-tubed, peach-pink, sweetly-scented flowers which open during the evening, each lasting a couple of days. It is relatively easy to grow, but does require regular fortnightly feeds during summer. H:15cm/6in; S:10cm/4in; WT:5°C/41°F; W:☼; S:☼; offsets, spring to mid-summer.

Ferocactus acanthodes (= *Echinocactus acanthodes*) (**2**), from Southern California, certainly lives up to its name, displaying sharp, tough, reddish spines up to 4cm/1½in long on a roundish body that becomes elongated with age. It is slow-growing, in its native country eventually reaching 1.8-3m/6-10ft high. In the home, however, it seldom reaches a fraction of this size. Small plants rarely flower and the 5cm/2in

3 **4**

long, yellow, mid-summer blooms are seldom seen. H:30-38cm/12-15in; S:15cm/6in; WT:5°C/41°F; W:☼; S:☼; seeds, mid-spring.

Mammillaria bocasana (**3**), from Mexico, is easy to grow, creating a domed plant formed of many small, blue-green heads, eventually creating a cushion adorned with silky-white spines. During early summer, it is freely covered with small, cream flowers that form circles around each head. H:15cm/6in; S:15cm/6in; WT:5°C/41°F; W:☼; S:☼; seeds, mid-spring to early summer.

Mammillaria zeilmanniana (**4**), from Mexico, is free-flowering, even on small plants. The 18mm/¾in wide, deep violet-red, flowers appear from early to mid-summer. H:5-6.5cm/2-2½in; S:13-15cm/5-6in; WT:5°C/41°F; W:☼; S:☼; seeds, mid-spring to early summer.

CACTUS FAMILY (contd) *Notocactus haselbergii* (**1**), from Brazil, has a flattened top to its globular stance, from which 4-5cm/1½-2in wide flowers appear during early summer. Unfortunately, young plants do not bear flowers. The ribs are densely covered in soft, whitish-yellow, spines. H:13-15cm/5-6in; S:10-13cm/4-5in; WT:5°C/41°F; W:☼; S:☼; seeds, spring.

Notocactus herteri(**2**), from South America, creates a large, globular body with reddish-brown spines and late summer, deep magenta, flowers. H:13-15cm/5-6in; S:15cm/6in; WT:5°C/41°F; W:☼; S:☼; seeds, spring.

Notocactus mammulosus (**4**), from Uruguay and Argentina, is an easily grown cacti for the home, and has the blessing of flowering at a young stage, with mid to late summer yellow blooms that display purplish centres. H:10-13cm/4-5in; S:7.5-10cm/3-4in; WT:5°C/41°F; W:☼; S:☼; seeds, spring.

Notocactus ottonis (**3**), from South America, forms an attractive clump, freely covered with slender, yellow spines. From early to mid-summer it bears small clusters of 6.5cm/2½in wide yellow flowers. H:10cm/4in; S:10-18cm/4-7in; WT:5°C/41°F; W:☼; S:☼; seeds, spring.

Opuntia microdasys (**5**), from Mexico, is slow-growing, with many branches formed of 7.5-15cm/3-6in long oval pads. These are attractively dotted with yellow, barbed bristles. It seldom develops its yellow flowers in the home. Like other plants in this genus,

it is ideal for setting at the back of a floor-standing arrangement of cacti. H:60-90cm/2-3ft; H:45-60cm/1½-2ft; WT:7-10°C/45-50°F; W:☼; S:☼; seeds, spring; cuttings, mid-summer.

CACTUS FAMILY (contd) ***Opuntia robusta*** (**1**) comes
from Mexico, where it often reaches 4.5-5.4m/15-
18ft, but in the home displays a restrained nature. Its
bluish-green, circular and flattened pads, about
20cm/8in long, are sparsely peppered with yellow
spines. Small plants do not flower. H:45-60cm/1½-
2ft; W:30-38cm/12-15in; WT:3-5°C/38-41°F; W:☼;
S:☼; seeds, spring; cuttings, mid-summer.

Opuntia scheerii (**2**) creates dull, blue-green,
15cm/6in long and 5cm/2in wide, flattened pads. In
Mexico it develops tree-like proportions, but in the
home has a more manageable size, with pads

peppered with golden spines and hairs. In the wild, it develops yellow flowers but in cultivation seldom blooms. H:60-90cm/2-3ft; S:38-45cm/15-18in; WT:7°C/45°F/ W:☼; S:☼; seeds, spring; cuttings, mid-summer.

Rebutia krainziana calliantha (= *R. calliantha*) (3), from South America, is beautiful in spring, when covered with rings of orange to red flowers. These are complimented by the short, white spines on the individual bodies that form the plant. It grows well on a sunny window-sill in a kitchen. H:10cm/4in; S:10-13cm/4-5in; WT:5°C/41°F; W:☼; S:☼; seeds, spring; offsets, summer.

Rebutia senilis (4), from Argentina, is a diminutive cacti, ideal for even the smallest window-sill. It forms a clump, with rings of showy, bright red, 18mm/³⁄₄in wide, flowers in late spring and early summer. H:5-10cm/2-4in; S:13-25cm/5-10in; WT:5°C/41°F; W:☼; S:☼; seeds, spring; offsets, summer.

CACTUS FAMILY (contd) **Easter Cactus** *Rhipsalidopsis gaertneri (= Epiphyllum russellianum/Schlumbergera gaertneri)* (**1**), from Southern Brazil, is best seen in an indoor hanging-basket or on the edge of a shelf, where the pendulous flowers can be fully enjoyed. It is often confused with the Christmas Cacti, *Schlumbergera hybrida*, but usually forms a much larger plant. Also, the Easter Cactus has stems which, although mainly flat, may have three to five angles. Bright red, 6.5cm/2½in wide, flowers appear from

early to late spring. H:38-45cm/15-18in; S:75-90cm/2½-3ft; WT:13°C/55°F; W:○-◐; S:◐-●; cuttings, summer, but some plants are grafted.

Christmas Cactus *Schlumbergera hybrida* (= *S.* x *buckleyi*) (**2**) is a cross between the Crab Cactus *Schlumbergera truncata* and *Schlumbergera russelliana*. It is well-known for its branching flat stems, with joints every 5cm/2in. The 5-7.5cm/2-3in long and 3cm/1¼in wide, unscented, mid to late winter, flowers appear at the ends of the stems. The usual colour is magenta, but pink and white forms are also available. The plant is best seen in an indoor hanging-basket or at the edge of a shelf where the stems can spread and droop. H:15-20cm/6-8in; S:23-25cm/9-10in; WT:13°C/55°F; W:○-◐; S:◐-●; cuttings, summer, but some plants are grafted.

Crab Cactus *Schlumbergera truncata* (= *Epiphyllum truncatum/Zygocactus truncatus*) (**3**), from Brazil, is often confused with the Christmas Cactus, which also has flattened stems. With the Crab Cactus these are longer, 5-7.5cm/2-3in, bright green at first and becoming red. The 5-7.5/2-3in long flowers appear slightly earlier, from early to mid-winter, primarily pink to deep red but also in shades of crimson, purple, blue and white. It is best seen growing in an indoor hanging-basket or at the edge of a shelf. H:20-30cm/8-12in; S:30-38cm/12-15in; WT:13°C/55°F; W:○-◐; S:◐-●; cuttings, summer, but some plants are grafted.

PEPPER FAMILY **Water-melon Plant** or **Water-melon Begonia** *Peperomia argyreia* (= *P. sandersii*) (**3**), from Brazil, is an outstandingly beautifully leaved plant. The leaves are spear-shaped and mainly silver-grey, but with green-banded veins. It needs careful watering during winter to avoid rotting of the bases of the red stems. It is ideal for placing on a low table, so that the leaves can be admired from above. H:15-20cm/6-8in; S:15-23cm/6-9in; WT:13°C/55°F; W:○; S:◉-◉; cuttings, spring to late summer.

Peperomia caperata (**1**), from tropical America, is a neat plant for the home, displaying attractively corrugated leaves. From late spring to mid-winter it reveals 13-15cm/5-6in long, pure white and antler-like flower spikes. Although widely grown, it is not the most attractive peperomia, but does well as a tone and colour relief for other houseplants, especially during winter. H:13-25cm/5-10in; S:13-18cm/5-7in; WT:10°C/50°F; W:○; S:◉-◉; cuttings, spring to late summer.

Ivy Peperomia *Peperomia griseoargentea* (= *P. hederifolia*) (**2**), from Brazil, is also known as Platinum Peperomia and Silver-leaf Peperomia. It very much resembles *P. caperata*, but has larger leaves, quilted and up to 6.5cm/2½in long. It, too, is useful when arranged with other plants. H:13-18cm/5-7in; S:15-20cm/6-8in; WT:10°C/50°F; W:○; S:◉-◉; cuttings, spring to late summer.

PEPPER FAMILY (contd) **Desert Privet** *Peperomia magnoliifolia* (**1**), from San Domingo, creates colour with its 5cm/2in long green leaves, but is best seen in a variegated form such as 'Variegata', displaying cream variegations, and 'Green Gold', with cream edges to the leaves. Eventually, these plants are bushy and much branched, creating a dominant display, either on their own or mixed with other plants. H:15-20cm/6-8in; S:20-25cm/8-10in; WT:10°C/50°F; W:○; S:◎-◐; cuttings, spring to late summer.

Baby Rubber Plant *Peperomia obtusifolia* (**3**), from tropical South America, is also known as the American Rubber Plant and Pepper-face. It is similar to *P. magnoliifolia*, but slightly hardier. From mid-summer to autumn it produces whitish flower spikes. H:15-23cm/6-9in; S:25-30cm/10-12in; WT:10°C/50°F; W:○; S:◎-◐; cuttings, spring to late summer.

Cupid Peperomia *Peperomia serpens* (= *P. scandens*) (**2**), from South America, is widely grown as a trailing or climbing plant, when the heart-shaped 5cm/2in long leaves create a spectacular display. It is superb when trailing from a high shelf or when in an indoor hanging-basket. It is usually seen in a variegated form, displaying green and cream leaves. H:1.2-1.5m/4-5ft - climbing; WT:13-16°C/55-61°F; W:○; S:◎-◐; cuttings, spring to late summer.

TRUMPET LEAF FAMILY **Pitcher Plant** *Sarracenia purpurea* (**1**) is from North America, where it is descriptively known as Sweet Pitcher Plant, Side-saddle Flower, Huntsman's-cup, Trumpet Leaf, Indian Cup and Devil's Boots, is an insectivorous plant that needs a cool room, greenhouse or conservatory during winter and must be grown in moisture-retentive compost. It is evergreen and displays green and purple pitcher-like heads, up to 5cm/2in wide. These contain a sugary material at their necks which attracts insects that then fall into a liquid at the base of the pitcher. There they drown and are digested by the plant. Downward-pointing hairs inside the pitcher prevent insects escaping. During spring, it develops greenish-purple 6.5-7.5cm/2½-3in wide flowers on long stems that tower above the pitchers. H:23cm/9in; S:25-30cm/10-12in; WT:5°C/41°F; W:☼-○; S:◐-●; seeds, early spring; division, early to mid-summer.

SUNDEW FAMILY **Venus Fly Trap** *Dionaea muscipula* (**2**) comes from boggy coastal areas in North and South Carolina in North America. It has jaw-like traps at the ends of its flattened leaves, often 13cm/5in long when mature. The traps are normally open and when an insect - usually a fly - steps on the jaw parts and disturbs one of the sensitive trigger hairs the trap closes. The plant then digests the insect with its digestive juices. Flowering weakens a plant, and therefore these are best pinched out. It grows well on a window-sill in the kitchen, where it creates a great

deal of interest. During those times when flies are not around, feed the plant every two to three weeks with a weak liquid fertilizer. H:7.5-13cm/3-5in; S:10-15cm/4-6in; WT:7-10°C/45-50°F; W:○; S:◎-◉; division, spring, as soon as growth starts; leaf-cuttings, spring to early summer.

STONECROP FAMILY **Crassula aborescens** (= *C. cotyledon/Cotyledon arborescens*) (**1**), from Cape Province, South Africa, is a succulent plant that develops into a shrub with grey-green leaves edged red. It is ideal for positioning at the back of a group of houseplants, especially near a large patio window. In the home it seldom bears its early to mid-summer white flowers that slowly become red. H:0.9-1.2m/3-4ft; S:0.9-1.2m/3-4ft; WT:5-7°C/41-45°F; W:☼; S:☼-○; seeds, late spring to early summer; stem-

1

cuttings, late spring to mid-summer; leaf-cuttings, spring and summer.

Crassula deceptor (= *C. deceptrix*) (**2**), from South Africa, is outstandingly attractive. The bell-shaped, white flowers appear in small clusters from late autumn to early winter. H:5-7.5cm/2-3in; S:10-15cm/4-6in; WT:7-10°C/45-50°F; W:☼; S:☼-◐; seeds, late spring to early summer; leaf-cuttings, spring and summer.

Crassula perfoliata falcata (= *C. falcata/Rochea falcata*) (**3**), from Cape Province, South Africa, is best known as *C. falcata*. It is a beautiful succulent, with mid to late summer, 7.5cm/3in wide heads of bright scarlet, bell-shaped flowers. H:30-60cm/1-2ft; S:23-38cm/9-15in; WT:7°C/45°F; W:☼; S:☼-◐; leaf-cuttings, spring and summer; seeds, late spring to early summer.

STONECROP FAMILY (contd) **Painted Lady** or **Baby Echeveria** *Echeveria derenbergii* (**1**), from Mexico, forms a stemless rosette, with offsets that create a cushion of attractive foliage. During summer, it develops upright, bell-shaped flowers on stems about 7.5cm/3in high. The insides of the flowers are yellow, with orange exteriors. H:5-7.5cm/2-3in; S:7.5-15in/3-6in - mat forming; WT:5°C/41°F; W:☼; S:☼-○; leaf-cuttings, spring to early summer; offsets, early spring.

Echeveria setosa (**3**), from Southern Mexico, is descriptively known in North America as the Mexican Fire Cracker or Firecracker Plant. It develops a flat, almost stemless rosette of leaves. H:7.5cm/3in; S:13-15cm/5-6in; WT:5°C/41°F; W:☼; W:☼-○; leaf-cuttings, spring to early summer; offsets, early spring.

Kalanchoe blossfeldiana (**2**), from Madagascar, is one of Nature's amenable and co-operative plants. Its natural inclination is to flower from mid-winter to early summer, but by giving this succulently-leaved plant periods of light and dark - at the same time providing a warm and uniform temperature - nurserymen can induce it to flower at any time of year. The normal type bears dense clusters of 12-25mm/½-1in long, tubular, scarlet, long lasting flowers, but white, yellow, pink and red forms are also available. H:20-30cm/8-12in; S:15-25cm/6-10in; WT:5-7°C/41-45°F; W:☼; S:○-◎; seeds, early spring.

1

STONECROP FAMILY (contd) ***Kalanchoe daigremontiana*** *(= Bryophyllum daigremontianum)* (**1**), from
Madagascar, is best known under its synonym. It is
a succulent plant with leaves bearing plantlets along
their edges. Children - and adults - find the plant
interesting, as when pressed into compost the small
plantlets soon develop roots. It is ideal for growing on
a sunny window-sill, and makes a reliable plant for an
office window, where it tolerates considerable
neglect. H:45-75cm/1½-2½ft; S:20-25cm/8-10in;
WT:10-12°C/50-54°F; W:☼; S:○-◉; plantlets from
leaves, spring and summer.

Kalanchoe pumila (**2**), from Madagascar, is a dwarf
and semi-prostrate succulent houseplant, ideal in an
indoor hanging-basket or in a pot positioned on an
inverted flower pot. It is useful for creating winter

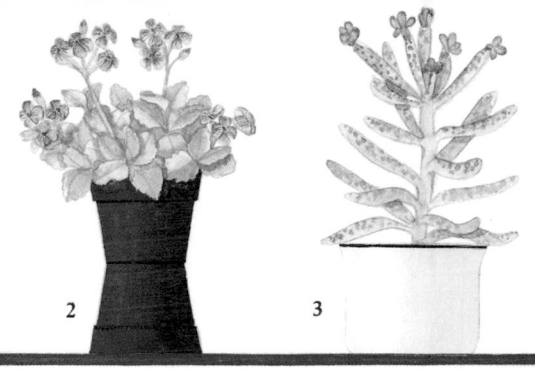

2

3

colour, as well as bringing year-through interest with foliage displaying a grey and waxy bloom. H:20çm/ 8in; S:20-30cm/8-12in. compt moisture and trailing; WT:8-/ 20/14-?? ?; W:?; S:☼ ☽, seeds, early spring, stem-cuttings, early to late summer.

Kalanchoe tubiflora *(= Bryophyllum tubiflorum)* (**3**), from Madagascar, is a succulent plant, best known under its synonym. Its central, stiff stem radiates cylindrical leaves, with clusters of plantlets at their ends. When pressed into compost they soon root. Like *Kalanchoe daigremontiana*, its easy and novel method of propagation is of special interest to young people. A sunny window-sill makes it a good home, and it does well in offices. H:45-75cm/1½-2½ft; S:15-20cm/6-8in; WT:10-12°C/50-54°; W:☼; S:○-◎; plantlets from the leaves, spring and summer.

81

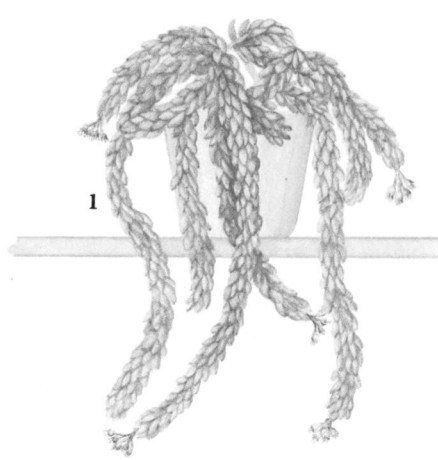

1

STONECROP FAMILY (contd) **Donkey's Tail, Beaver Tail** or **Burro's Tail** *Sedum morganianum* (**1**), from Mexico, is superb in an indoor hanging-basket, or positioned to trail from a high shelf. The tail-like, 30-75cm/1-2½ft long, stems are densely clustered with 18mm/¾in long and 9mm/1/3in wide fleshy, grey-green leaves that look superb when trailing freely. From mid to late summer, the ends of the stems are clustered with pale rose-pink flowers, but only on mature plants. Trailing stems up to 75cm/2½ft long; WT:5°C/41°F; W:☼○; S:○-◉; seeds, spring; leaf-cuttings, spring and summer.

Sedum rubrotinctum (**3**), from Mexico, creates a mass of small, fleshy, bright green leaves. They cluster along the stems, bending them down until they touch the compost. During summer, it bears clusters of yellow flowers. H:15-20cm/6-8in; S:20-30cm/8-12in; WT:5°C/41°F; W:☼-○; S:○-◉; seeds, spring; leaf-cuttings, spring and summer.

Sedum sieboldii '**Medio-variegatum**' (**2**), from Japan, is ideal for an indoor hanging-basket or where it can trail freely. The spreading stems, with flat, rounded leaves striped white, look best when spread out. During early autumn, it bears 5-7.5cm/2-3in wide flat clusters of pink flowers. H:5-7.5cm/2-3in; S:30-38cm/12-15in and semi-trailing; WT:5°C/41°F; W:☼-○; S:○-◉; stem-cuttings, spring and summer.

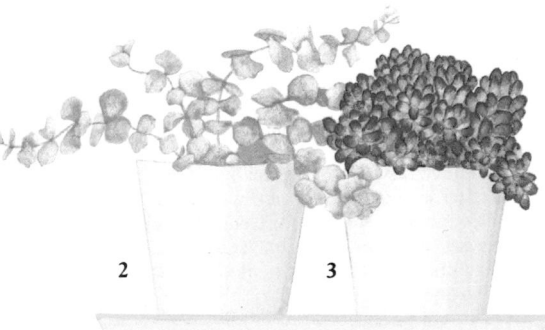

2   3

SAXIFRAGE FAMILY **Common Hydrangea** or **House Hydrangea** *Hydrangea macrophylla* (**1**), from China and Japan, is a hardy shrub that creates large heads of blue, pink and white flowers in the garden during mid to late summer. Young plants can be grown in pots and induced to flower indoors during summer. Strong-growing plants, rooted and well established the previous summer, are given temperatures between 7-10°C/45-50°F during mid-winter. Keep the compost moist and they flower without too much trouble. After flowering, plant them in a border and use fresh plants the following year. Any plants that are kept should be pruned hard back and repotted into a larger container and stood outdoors until being re-started into growth. A cool period at this stage is essential. The acidity of the compost influences the colouring of pink and blue varieties. Pink can be make blue by using acid compost. H:30-45cm/1-1½ft in pots; 25-38cm/10-15in in pots; WT:7-10°C/45-50°F; W:○; S:◉; cuttings, late summer.

Mother of Thousands *Saxifraga stolonifera* (= *S. sarmentosa*) (**2**), from eastern Asia, is known in North America as the Strawberry Geranium, Beefsteak Geranium, Strawberry Begonia and Creeping Sailor. It is ideal in a pot positioned where the thread-like runners can trail for several feet. The large, circular leaves are the main attraction. It has white flowers at mid-summer. The form 'Tricolor' displays pink and light yellow variegated leaves. H:23-30cm/9-12in; S:25-30cm/10-12in and trailing; WT:4°C/39°F; W:○;

S:◎; division, spring to early summer; rooted runners, spring and summer.

1

2

SAXIFRAGE FAMILY (contd) **Pig-a-back Plant, Thousand Mothers** or **Youth on Age** *Tolmiea menziesii* (**1**) gains further names from its native Western North America, such as Pickaback and Piggyback Plant. The names aptly describe the plantlets that grow from the points where the leaf-stalks join the hairy maple-like leaves, especially on mature plants. These plantlets create great interest for children, as they can be easily rooted by pegging the whole leaf into a box of compost. In mid-summer it develops 45cm/1½ft high spikes of tubular, greenish-white flowers. It is hardy, easily grown, compact and clump-forming, ideal for cold and draughty places in the home. H:13-15cm/5-6in; S:30-38cm/12-15in; WT:hardy; W:○; S:◐-●; detach plantlets from leaves, spring and summer.

PEA FAMILY **Humble Plant** or **Sensitive Plant** *Mimosa pudica* (**2**) is a superb Brazilian shrub, usually grown as an annual and invariably of great interest to children. The plant is not particularly attractive, but the small leaflets along the central stems close up if touched. If the whole plant is knocked, the leaf stalks also collapse downwards, as if wilting. Plants may take up to an hour to recover completely before the performance can be repeated, but too frequent touchings may cause the total or long-term collapse of the plant. H:45-60cm/1½-2ft; S:30-38cm/12-15in; WT:18°C/64°F; W:☼-○; S:○-◐; seeds, late winter to early spring.

GERANIUM FAMILY **Scented-leaved Geranium** *Pelargonium crispum* (**1**), from South Africa, is well-known for its fragrant, crisped and notched leaves. Clusters of 2.5cm/1in wide pink flowers appear from early to late summer. For extra interest, try a variegated type. Many forms are available, in scents including lemon, orange, pepper, orange-lemon, pine and eucalyptus. It is ideal for hiding unpleasant cooking smells. H:45-75cm/1½-2½ft; S:38-45cm/15-18in; WT:7-10°C/45-50°F; W:☼; S:☼-◐; cuttings, mid to late summer.

Regal Pelargonium *Pelargonium* x *domesticum* (**2**) is an erect but branched plant, burgeoned with pink to purple 4-5cm/1½-2in wide flowers from early summer to autumn. The range of varieties is extensive, in a kaleidoscope of colour. It is ideal for brightening bedrooms. H:38-45cm/15-24in; S:30-38cm/12-15in; WT:7-10°C/45-50°F; W:☼; S:☼-○; cuttings, mid to late summer.

1

2

GERANIUMFAMILY (contd) **Zonal Pelargonium** *Pelargonium* x *hortorum* (**1**) is distinquished by its large, rounded leaves with contrasting chocolate-brown zones. The early summer to autumn flowers are eye-catching, in a wide colour range of named varieties. It is sun-loving, so try it on sunny window-sills. H:0.6-1m/2-3½ft; S:38-75cm/15-45cm; WT:7-10°C/45-50°F; W:☼; S:☼-○; cuttings, mid to late summer.

Ivy-leaved Geranium *Pelargonium peltatum* (**2**), from South Africa, displays beautiful, trailing stems up to 90cm/3ft long. It is best grown in an indoor hanging-basket or positioned on a pedestal, where the stems can trail. Alternatively, grow it in pots placed in wall brackets, and positioned either side of patio windows. It displays 2.5cm/1in wide carmine-pink flowers from early to late summer. Many named forms are available, with double, semi-double and single flowers in colours including white, mauve, purple and pink. Trailing stems; WT:7-10°C/45-50°F; W:☼; S:☼-○; cuttings, mid to late summer.

FLAX FAMILY **Yellow Flax Plant** *Reinwardtia indica*
(= *R. trigyna*/*R. tetragyna*) (**3**), from Northern India,
is an attractive evergreen shrub with bright yellow,
funnel-shaped, 2.5-4cm/1-1½in long flowers from
autumn to early spring. It eventually needs a
greenhouse or conservatory. In the home, fresh plants
are best raised each year. To keep them dwarf and
bushy, pinch out the growing tips several times.
H:45-60cm/1½-2ft; S:38-45cm/15-18in; WT:13°C/
55°F; W:☼ S:○; cuttings, mid-spring.

SPURGE FAMILY **Red Hot Cat's Tail** *Acalpha hispida*
(= *A. sanderi*) (**1**), native to the Malay archipelago, is
known in North America as Chenille Plant, Foxtail
and Philippine Medusa. Young plants in small pots
create an impressive display in the home, but in a
conservatory, they grow to3m/10ft or more high. The
massed, tail-like red flowers, up to 5cm/2cm long,
appear during summer and are best seen on large
plants. H:60-90cm/2-3ft in the home; S:45-60cm/
1½-2ft in the home; WT:16-18°C/61-64°F; W:☼;
S:○-◉; cuttings, late summer.

Joseph's Coat or **Croton** *Codiaeum variegatum pictum*
(**2**), from Malaysia, is a superb foliage plant for the
home, displaying leaves in many shapes and bright
colours. In a greenhouse these plants often reach
2.4-3m/8-10ft, but in pots in the home are less
vigorous. Many distinctive colour forms are available,
such as 'Carrierei' with yellow-green leaves that
mature to reveal red centres, 'Reidii' with bold cream
veins and laurel-like leaves, 'Disraeli' displaying

slender mid-green leaves blotched creamy-yellow above and 'Holuffiana' with cream veining on forked leaves. Good light brings out the full beauty of the leaves. H:45-60cm/1½-2ft; S:30-45cm/1-1½ft; WT:13-15°C/55-59°F; W:☼-○; S:○-◎; cuttings, early spring to mid-summer.

SPURGE FAMILY (contd) **Crown of Thorns** *Euphorbia milii* (= *E. splendens*) (**1**), from Madagascar, is known in North America as Christ Thorn and Christ Plant. It gains its religious associations from the spiny, semi-prostrate stems that bear crimson, kidney-shaped bracts throughout the year and especially during winter. It is best kept away from the reach of

young children, who might harm themselves on the thorns. H:30-60cm/1-2ft; S:30-60cm/1-2ft; WT:13°C/55°F; W:☼; S:☼-○; cuttings, mid-summer.

Euphorbia obesa (**2**), from Cape Province, reveals a superb spherical body that, with age, becomes cylindrical. The body bears eight ribs and develops delicately scented, tiny, white flowers clustered at their tops during summer. H:15-25cm/6-10in; S:7.5-13cm/3-5in; WT:5°C/41°F; W:☼; S:☼-○; seeds, early spring.

Poinsettia *Euphorbia pulcherrima* (**3**), from Mexico, is sold in millions just before Christmas, when adorned with coloured, leaf-like bracts up to 15cm/6in long, usually red but also in pink, white and cream. Few plants can compete with the colourful impact of this winter brightener. The plants are frequently treated with chemicals to keep them compact and dwarf, as well as given artificial periods of light and darkness to control their flowering period. Therefore, once flowered the plants are best discarded and fresh ones bought the following year. At one time the coagulating juice produced by some euphorbias was used to prevent the formation of rust on the bottoms of ships. In 1873, in a British dockyard experiment, a sheet of iron was coated in latex and submerged in water for two years. Little corrosion occurred and four years later the Protector Fluid Company was formed to manufacture the latex paint. The discovery of this property of *Euphorbia* juice is said to have been made accidentally when cutting plants of the Euphorbia family in Natal, South Africa. The juice was found to adhere firmly to the blades of knives, preventing rust forming on the metal. As well as preventing the formation of rust on the hulls of metal ships, the juice also prevents the adhesion of barnacles. This reduces the cost of frequent cleaning and assisted in the maintenance of speed on fast-going vessels of that era. H:0.75-90cm/2½-3ft; S:30-38cm/12-15in; WT:18°C/64°F; W:◎; S:◉; cuttings, spring to early summer.

1

BALSAM FAMILY **Busy Lizzie** *Impatiens walleriana (=
I. holstii)* (**1**) now includes *I. sultani*, formerly a
separate species. Irrespective of how botanists classify
these East African and Zanzibar plants they are ideal
for spring to early autumn flowers in a colour range
including bright scarlet, white, magenta and crimson.
Individual plants are often grown for too long and
create a straggly mass of bare stems with a few leaves
and flowers at their tops. It is best to grow
replacements from cuttings each year so that plants in
the autumn of their years can be discarded and
replaced with younger types. Several compact and
free-flowering hybrid varieties are available, ideal as
pot plants. Some are superb in indoor hanging-
baskets, but they all thrive on sunny window-sills.
These hybrids can be raised from seeds. The Busy
Lizzie *I. sultani* was introduced into Britain from
Zanzibar in 1896 by the famous botanist Joseph
Hooker, who, like his father before him, was Director
of the Royal Botanic Garden at Kew. He named the
plant in honour of the Sultan of Zanzibar.

Impatiens plants have collected a wide range of
amusing common names. *I. balsamina*, from tropical
Asia, is widely known as Jumping Betty, Touch-me-
not and Balsam. In North America it is known as the
Garden Balsam and Rose Balsam. The much larger *I.
glandulifera*, previously *I. roylei*, is known as the
Himalayan Balsam and Policeman's Helmet. H:45-
60cm/1½-2ft; S:38-45cm/15-18in; WT:10-13°C/50-
55°F; W:○; S:○-◉; cuttings, spring to late summer;
seeds, early spring.

VINE FAMILY **Kangaroo Vine** *Cissus antarctica* (**1**), from Australia is a well-known evergreen climber for the home, especially suitable for cool halls and the sides of windows, where it can be trained to create a living framework, or perhaps scrambling over a room divider. It grows well even in cool and gloomy positions, in hallways and on landings. The sharply-toothed leaves are up to 10cm/4in long. H:1.8-

2.4m/6-8ft in a 15-20cm/6-8in wide pot; climber; WT:7-10°C/45-50°F; W:○; S:◎-●; cuttings, early to mid-summer.

VINE FAMILY (contd) **Begonia Vine** *Cissus discolor* (**2**), from the East Indies and known in North America by the descriptive common names Trailing Begonia, Climbing Begonia, Rex-begonia Vine and Begonia Cissus, is not so hardy as the previous species. During winter it tends to shed some leaves and become semi-evergreen. As well as being grown as a climber, it can be planted in an indoor hanging-basket, or in a pot positioned at the edge of a shelf, where it will trail. H:1.5-2.5m/5-8ft in a pot indoors; climber; WT:13-16°C/55-61°F; W:○; S:◎-●; cuttings, early to mid-spring.

Grape Ivy *Rhoicissus rhomboidea* (= *Cissus rhombifolia*) (**3**), from Natal, is a vigorous evergreen climber, often confused with the Kangaroo Vine. The Grape Ivy has leaves formed of three, irregular-edged, diamond-shaped leaflets, whereas on the Kangaroo Vine they are oval, pointed, tooth-edged and borne singly. Also, the Grape Ivy clings by means of tendrils, while the Kangaroo Vine lacks these and needs training and securing to canes or other supports. In a greenhouse border it may reach 4.5-6m/15-20ft, but in a pot indoors is less vigorous. H:1.2-1.8m/4-6ft in a pot indoors; climber; WT:7-10°C/45-50°F; W:○; S:◎-●; cuttings, late spring to early summer.

LIME FAMILY **African Hemp, House Lime** or **African Windflower** *Sparmannia africana* (**1**), from South Africa, can be grown in a pot in the home, conservatory or greenhouse. From early to mid-summer it reveals 2.5cm/1in wide heads of white, fragrant flowers with bright centres. Eventually the plant becomes too large for the home. A position near to a large window suits it best. H:45-60cm/1½-2ft in pots; S:30-38cm/12-15in in pots; WT:7°C/45°F; W:○; S:○-◉; cuttings, mid-spring.

MALLOW FAMILY **Abutilon x hybridum** (**2**) is a well-branched shrub, ideal for a greenhouse border where it reaches 1.8-2.4m/6-8ft high and with a spread up to 1.5m/5ft. In a pot it reaches about half this size, but nevertheless is highly attractive and very useful as a background for a group of floor-standing houseplants. The maple-like, three to five-lobed,

1

mid-green leaves are part of the attraction, with the bonus of 4cm/1½in long pendent flowers from early to late summer. There are several superb varieties, two good ones being 'Ashford Red', with salmon-red flowers, and 'Golden Fleece', yellow. H:0.6-1.2m/2-4ft; S:45-75cm/1½-2½ft; WT:5-7°C/41-45°F; W:○; S:○-◎; cuttings, early to late summer.

***Abutilon striatum* 'Thompsonii'** (= *A. thompsonii*) (**3**), from Brazil, is another tender shrub. In a greenhouse it is large, but indoors it is more manageable. It is mainly grown for its maple-like, three to five-lobed leaves, beautifully mottled yellow. From early to late summer it bears 4cm/1½in long, orange and crimson flowers. H:0.6-1m/2-3½ft; S:45-60cm/1½-2ft; WT:5-7°C/41-45°F; W:○; S:○-◎; cuttings, early to late summer.

MALLOW FAMILY (contd) **Chinese Rose** *Hibiscus rosa-sinensis* (**1**), from China, is an eye-catching shrub, primarily for warm greenhouses, although it will survive in the home at lower temperatures. From mid-summer to autumn it bears short-lived, 13cm/5in wide, flowers from the upper leaf joints. Normally, the flowers are single and crimson, but semi-double and double forms are available. The dwarf and compact form 'Cooperi' is excellent in pots in the home, displaying crimson flowers and variegated foliage. Hibiscus flowers contain astrigent juice and when bruised turn black or deep purple. This juice was used by Chinese ladies to dye hair and eyebrows. In Java it was used for blacking shoes and called the Shoe-black Plant. In North America it is known as the Blacking Plant. H:0.9-1.8m/3-6ft; S:0.75-1.5m/2½-5ft; WT:7-10°C/45-50°F; W:☼; S:○-◎; cuttings, spring to late summer.

RUE FAMILY **Calamondin** *Citrus microcarpa* (= *C. mitis*) (**2**), from the Philippines, is the best species of citrus for growing in pots indoors or in conservatories and greenhouses. It is dwarf and at an early stage in its growth bears flowers and fruits over a long period. Fragrant, 12mm/½in wide, white flowers are followed by 2.5cm/1-1½in wide, sour but edible, fruits that soon turn to a rich orange. The fruits can be preserved in syrup and used for desserts. H:75-90cm/2½-3ft; S:45-60cm/1½-2ft; WT:10-13°C/50-55°F; W:☼; S:☼-○; seeds, early spring; cuttings, mid to late summer.

1

2

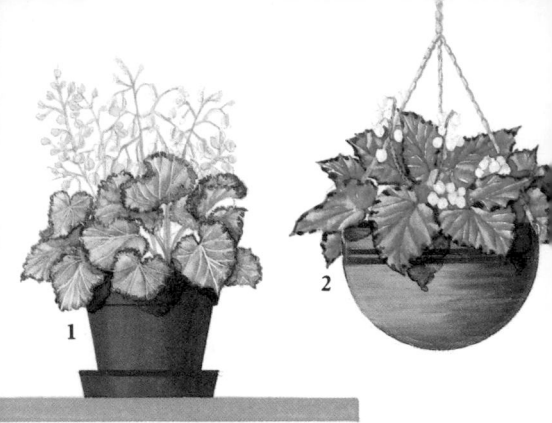

BEGONIA FAMILY **Eye-lash Begonia** *Begonia boweri*
(**2**), from Mexico, presents an impressive display of
small, chocolate-brown edged, bright green leaves,
from late winter to late spring surmounted by
12mm/½in wide white or pink flowers. H:15-
23cm/6-9in; S:20-30cm/8-12in; WT:13°C/55°F;
W:○; W:◉; division, spring; cuttings, early to
mid-summer.

Begonia manicata (**1**), a rhizomatous begonia, from
Mexico, creates an impressive display of pink flowers,
up to 12mm/½in wide, from mid-winter to early
spring. The mid-green leaves have tufts of red hairs
on their undersides. H:38-45cm/15-18in; S:38-45cm/
15-18in; WT:10°C/50°F; W:○; S:◉; cuttings, early
to mid-summer.

Iron Cross Begonia *Begonia masoniana* (**3**), from South-east Asia, grown for its mid-green, corrugated leaves, emblazed with bronze-purple bars. H:20-25cm/8-10in; S:25-30cm/10-12in; WT:13°C/55°F; W:○; S:◎; leaf cuttings, early to mid-summer.

Begonia metallica (**4**), from Brazil, is fibrous-rooted and well known for the metallic sheen on its leaves. The 12-18mm/½-¾in wide pink-flushed white flowers appear during early autumn. It is sturdy and decorative, large enough to be placed in a cluster of house plants near a patio window. H:60-75cm/2-2½ft; S:45-60cm/1½-2ft; WT:10°C/50°F; W:○; S:◎; stem-cuttings, early to late summer.

BEGONIA FAMILY (contd) **Begonia Rex** (**1**), from Assam, is a rhizomatous type grown for its large, arrow-shaped and colourful leaves. Several forms are available, with varying coloration. Infrequently, 12mm/½in wide pale pink flowers appear from mid-summer to early autumn, but these are best removed to encourage the development of more leaves. H:23-30cm/9-12in; S:30-38cm/12-15in; WT:13°C/55°F; W:○; S:◎; division, spring; leaf-cuttings, early to mid-summer.

Elephant's Ear *Begonia scharffii (= B. haageana)* (**2**), from Brazil, is a shrubby, fibrous-rooted begonia, with deep green leaves with purplish-red undersides. Clusters of 2.5cm/1in wide, pink-tinged white flowers appear from mid-summer to early autumn. Placed on the floor, it makes a background for smaller

1

plants.   H:0.75-1m/2½-3½ft;   S:45-60cm/1½-2ft; WT:10°C/50°F; W:○; S:◉; stem-cuttings, early to late summer.

Wax Begonia *Begonia semperflorens* (**3**), a well-known fibrous type from Brazil, is highly floriferous, bearing red, pink or white flowers up to 2.5cm/1in wide from early to late summer and even into early autumn. Its hybrids are widely seen. Most gardeners know this as a summer-bedding plant, but it grows well on window-sills shaded by net curtains. H:15-23cm/6-9in; S:15-23cm/6-9in; WT:16°C/61°F - for seed sowing; W:○; S:◉; seeds, late winter to mid-spring.

3

BEGONIA FAMILY (contd) ***Begonia x tuberhybrida*** (**3**) is a spectacular tuberous-rooted hybrid with beautiful 7.5-15cm/3-6in wide flowers from early to late summer. Named forms available includie 'Festiva' (yellow), 'Olympia' (crimson), 'Diana Wynyard' (white), 'Harlequin' (white, edged pink), 'Rosanna' (rose-pink) and there are many others. It is superb for any bright position. H:30-60cm/1-2ft; S:30-38cm/12-15in; WT:18°C/64°F; W:○; S:◎; tubers, plant in shallow boxes or pots during early to mid-spring.

LOOSESTRIFE FAMILY **Cigar Flower** or **Mexican Cigar Flower** *Cuphea ignea* (**2**), from Mexico, is an ideal evergreen shrub for the home. Eventually, it grows large and is best positioned in a conservatory. In North America it is known as the Firecracker Plant. These names aptly describe the colourful, massed, late spring to early winter, 2.5cm/1in long, bright scarlet, tubular flowers. Plants kept for a second year need trimming back by one-half to two-thirds in early spring. H:30-38cm/12-15in in small pots; S:30-38cm/12-15in; WT:7°C/45°F; W:☼-○; S:◎-●; seeds, late winter; cuttings, early to mid-spring.

POMEGRANATE FAMILY **Dwarf Pomegranate** *Punica granatum* 'Nana' (**1**), from Iran and Afghanistan, makes a better house plant than the normal Pomegranate, (*Punica granatum*), which eventually reaches 2.4-3m/8-10ft high. It is also hardier and bushier. It is chiefly grown for its tubular, bright scarlet, early to late summer, flowers – followed by tiny fruits, resembling miniature pomegranates. It enjoys a really sunny position, so place it near to a window. H:45-75cm/1½-2½ft; S:45-60cm/1½-2ft; WT:5-7°C/41-45°F; W:☼; S:☼; seeds, early spring; cuttings, mid-summer.

IVY FAMILY **Umbrella Tree** *Brassaia actinophylla* (= *Schefflera actinophylla*) (**2**) is a tropical evergreen from Polynesia, displaying spear-shaped leaves in an umbrella-like arrangement. Young plants do not exhibit as many leaflets as older specimens. It is slow-growing and eventually needs a large pot, and forms an ideal foliage plant for a large corner. It looks best when positioned with a plain, light-coloured background. H:1.8-2.4m/6-8ft; S:60-90cm/2-3ft; WT:10-13°C/50-55°F; W:○; S:◉; seeds, late winter to early spring.

False Aralia or **Spider Plant** *Dizygotheca elegantissima* (= *Aralia elegantissima*) (**3**) is an elegant evergreen tree from the New Hebrides. In its juvenile and houseplant form, it develops a straight-stem with elegant, spider-like, reddish foliage. When about 1.5m/5ft high, the foliage broadens, losing its graceful form. Plants at this height can be cut back in spring to encourage fresh shoots. It is ideal for filling large corners or walls, or even for creating part of a plant partition within a room. H:0.9-1.5/3-5ft; S:38-45cm/15-18in; WT:13°C/55°F; W:○; S:◉-●; seeds, late winter to mid-spring.

Tree Ivy or **Climbing Figleaf** X *Fatshedera lizei* (**1**) is a cross between two plants belonging to different genera. The parents are *Fatsia japonica* 'Moseri', a form of the False Castor Oil Plant, and the Irish Ivy *Hedera helix* 'Hibernica'. The result is a sprawling, evergreen shrub with hand-like, five-lobed leaves. It can be trained as a climber. The form 'Variegata' is

highly attractive, its leaves edged with creamy-white, but it does need a brighter position than the green type, which grows well in shady and cool positions such as halls. H:1.2-1.8m/4-6ft; S:O.9-1.2m/3-4ft; WT:4-7°C/39-45°F; W:○-◎; S:◎-●; cuttings, mid to late summer.

1

2

IVY FAMILY (contd) **Canary Island Ivy** *Hedera canariensis* 'Variegata' (**2**) is a large-leaved ivy from North Africa and the Canary Islands that grows well outside in most temperate and sub-tropical areas. An attractive and hardy houseplant, outdoors reaching 4.5-6m/15-20ft high, indoors it stops growing when its alloted area has been filled. Its variegated leaves turn reddish during cold periods, adding to its beauty. Good for covering a room-dividing screen with foliage and an ideal plant for a hall or porch, it will tolerate dull places, but the lightly-coloured variegations may disappear in too dark positions. H:1.5-2.4m/5-8ft; climber; WT:2°C/35°F; W:○-◎; S:◎-; cuttings, mid to late summer.

Common Ivy *Hedera helix* (**3**), from Europe, has spawned many superb small-leaved forms for growing indoors. The all green types are best for placing in dark corners, the variegated forms needing more light if their colouring is not to be lost. H:30-45cm/1-1½ft; climber; WT:2°C/35°F; W:○-◎; S:◎-●; cuttings, mid to late summer.

Green Rays *Schefflera arboricola* (= *Heptapleurum arboricola*) (**1**), from South-east Asia, is compact and bushy, with leaves formed of nine slender leaflets. Ideal foliage for a bright corner. H:1.2-1.8/4-6ft; S:45-75cm/1½-2½ft; WT:10-13°C/50-55°; W:○; S:◎; seeds, late winter to early spring.

1

HEATH FAMILY **Indian Azalea** *Rhododendron simsii* (**1**), from China, is best known as the azalea that can be forced into flower during winter. Frequently, it is erroneously called *R. indicum*. It creates an impressive display in the home, but is not easy to grow. Plants are usually bought when in bud, with colour just peeping through, and they need a constant temperature and a position free from draughts. After flowering, they can be placed in a greenhouse or frost-proof shed and planted into the garden in spring. Many of them are disbudded by nurserymen, to encourage the development of extra large flowers, and if this has been done the plants are best discarded after flowering. H:45-60cm/1½-2ft; S:45-60cm/1½-2ft; WT:10-13°C/50-55°F; W:◒-◉; S:◎; buy fresh plants each year.

Erica gracilis (**2**), from South Africa, is a winter flowering greenhouse heather, often sold in small pots when just starting to flower. Its normal flowering is autumn to mid-winter, but nurseries manipulate temperatures for mid-winter flowering. In a cool position it lasts a long time in flower. H:30-38cm/12-15in; S:23-30cm/9-12in; WT:5°C/41°F; W:○; S:◎-◉; cuttings, early spring.

Cape Heath *Erica hiemalis* (**3**) is another winter heather, naturally flowering from early to mid-winter. Its native country is uncertain. If left in the border of a cool greenhouse it eventually reaches 60cm/2ft high, but is frequently sold in pots for house decoration. H:30-38cm/12-15in; S:23-30cm/8-12in; WT:5°C/41°F; W:○; S:◎-◉; cuttings, early spring.

MYRSINE FAMILY **Coral Berry** or **Spear Flower**
Ardisia crenata (= *A. crenulata/A.crispa*) (**2**), from the
East Indies, is known in North America as the
Spiceberry, refering to the long-lasting bright red
berries. The star-shaped and sweetly-scented flowers
appear during early summer, followed by berries. In
some seasons, the berries last until flowering time the
following year. H:60-90cm/2-3ft; S:30-45cm/1-1½ft;
WT:7°C/45°F; W:○; S:◎; seeds, early spring;
cuttings, early to late summer.

Alpine Violet *Cyclamen persicum* (**1**), from the eastern
Mediterranean, sold in millions from early autumn to
spring and especially during mid-winter. The
butterfly-like flowers - some fragrant - appear above
the rounded and marbled leaves. The plants are
usually bought when in bud or just coming into
flower. Widely fluctuating temperatures, hot and
stuffy rooms, draughts and water inadvertently
tipped on the flowers or the bases of the stems can
create problems. It is at its best when placed on a
coffee table, or a dining table when not in use. In
southern Europe the fleshy rootstocks of native
cyclamen have been greedily sought by swine, and
the plants have earned the name *Pane porcino* and
Pain de Porceau. At one time this led the English to
call all cyclamen Sowbread. H:15-23cm/6-9in; S:15-
25cm/6-10in; WT:10-13°C/50-55°F; W:○-◎; S:◎;
seeds, late summer to early autumn for plants to
flower 15 months later, or late winter for plants to
flower the following winter.

PRIMROSE FAMILY ***Primula* x *kewensis*** (**2**) originated at the world-famous Kew Gardens, and reveals delicate and fragrant whorls of yellow flowers from mid-winter to mid-spring. H:30-38cm/12-15in; S:20-25cm/8-10in; WT:7-10°C/45-50°F; W:○-◎; S:◎; seeds, early to mid-summer.

Fairy Primrose or **Baby Primrose** *Primula malacoides* (**1**), from China, displays star-like flowers from mid-winter to late spring. Varieties are in colours such as pink, carmine-red, white, lavender and white, with yellow eyes. Some are fragrant. H:30-45cm/1-1½ft; S:25-38cm/10-15in; WT:7-10°C/45-50°F; W:○-◎; S:◎; seed, early to mid-spring.

Primula obconica (**4**), from China, is another popular and well-known houseplant. The clustered flower heads appear from mid-winter to early summer, in a colour range including white, crimson, salmon-red and purple-blue. The attractive 2.5cm/1in wide flowers belie the leaves, which occasionally can cause a painful and itching, reddish skin. H:23-38cm/9-15in; S:20-25cm/8-10in; WT:7-10°C/45-50°F; W:○-◎; S:◎; seeds, early to mid-spring.

Chinese Primula *Primula praenitens* (= *P. sinensis*) (**3**), again from China, is another dull season brightener, with 2.5-4cm/1-1½in wide flowers in whorls from mid-winter to mid-spring. Like *P. obconica*, it can cause a rash. H:25cm/10in; S:15-20cm/6-8in; WT:7-10°C/45-50°F; W:○-◎ S:◎; seeds, early to mid-summer.

119

SEA-LAVENDER FAMILY **Cape Leadwort** *Plumbago auriculata (= P. capensis)* (**1**) is a climber from South

1

2

120

Africa. When grown in a greenhouse it grows to about 4.5m/15ft high, but if carefully trained and pruned makes a beautiful plant for the home. From mid-spring to early winter it reveals 23-30cm/9-12in long clusters of trumpet-shaped flowers, each 2.5cm/1in wide. After flowering, cut back the plant by two-thirds. It is an ideal plant for growing around a window frame. The word *wort* - part of the common name - indicates a medicinal association. The caustic roots of a related species, *Plumbago europaea*, have been used by beggars to raise ulcers on their bodies to excite pity and encourage donations to their finances. H:1.2-1.5m/4-5ft in a pot; S:45-60cm/1½-2ft in a pot; WT:7°C/45°F although slightly higher temperatures encourage a longer flowering period; W:○-◐; S:◐-◉; cuttings, early to mid-summer.

OLIVE FAMILY PINK JASMINE *Jasminum polyanthum* (2), from China, is a versatile climber, equally attractive trailing along wires in the roof of a greenhouse or conservatory as in a 13cm/5in wide pot in the home. Indoors, it is best trained over a 45-60cm/1½-2ft high loop of pliable canes, over which it can climb and sprawl. This also allows the plant to be moved to an out-of-the-way position when not in flower. From early winter to late spring, it creates a wealth of powerfully scented, white, tubular flowers, pink in bud, in lax clusters 5-13cm/2-5in long. H:1.0-1.5m/3½-5ft in a pot indoors; WT:10-13°C/50-55°F; W:☼-p; S:○-◉; cuttings, late summer to early autumn.

GENTIAN FAMILY **Persian Violet** *Exacum affine* (**1**) originated from the island of Socotra in the Arabian Sea, a few hundred miles off the coast of South Yemen. Perhaps a more precise name should have been Arabian Violet, although curiously in North America it is known as the German Violet. It is a fragrant, bushy and compact plant for the home, bringing colour from mid-summer to early autumn. It is usually bought when just showing colour and discarded when the flowers fade. H:23-30cm/9-12in; S:15-23cm/6-9in; WT:10-13°C/50-55°F; W:○; S:◎; seeds, early spring.

PERIWINKLE FAMILY **Common Allamanda** or **Golden Trumpet** *Allamanda cathartica*, (**2**) from South America, is a vigorous evergreen climber. In pots keep it small by frequently nipping out the growing

tips when the shoots are 23-30cm/9-12in long. 'Grandiflora' displays 7.5cm/3in long, trumpet-shaped, yellow flowers, 'Hendersonii' orange-yellow. Both flower mid-summer to early autumn. H:3-3.5m/10-12ft; S:1.8-2m/6-8ft; WT:13°C/55°F; W:☼-○; cuttings, mid-spring to early summer.

2

PERIWINKLE FAMILY (contd) **Madagascar Periwinkle**
Catharanthus roseus (= Vinca rosea) (**1**), from
Madagascar and widely through the tropics, is ideal
in the home, where it creates colour from spring to
early autumn with 2.5-4cm/1-1½in wide, rose-pink
flowers. Although a tender shrub, it is best raised
fresh each year. Plants can be increased from seeds or
cuttings. If one plant is grown as a perennial and
retained from season to season, cut it back in spring
and use the trimmings as cuttings. H:30-38cm/12-
15in; S:25-30cm/10-12in; WT:13°C/55°F; W:☼-○;
S:○-◎; seeds, early spring; cuttings, mid-spring.

Dipladenia splendens (= Mandevilla splendens), (**2**)
from Brazil, is a vigorous evergreen climber that
usually needs a permanent framework up which to
climb, when it will reach 3-4.5m/10-15ft. However, it
flowers at an early age and when only 23-30cm/9-12in
high. This enables it to be grown in the home. To
keep it small, trimming is necessary during early
summer. From early summer to early autumn it
develops 15-20cm/6-8in long heads of trumpet-
shaped flowers. H:0.9-1.5m/3-5ft; WT:13-16°C/55-
61°F; W:☼-○; S:☼-○; cuttings, early to mid-spring.

Oleander or **Rosebay** *Nerium oleander* (**3**) from
Mediterranean regions, grows outside in warm areas,
but elsewhere needs protection, either in a conservatory in a large tub, where it grows 1.8-3.5m/6-12ft
high, or indoors in a pot where its size is more
manageable. The terminal clusters of 2.5-4cm/1-

1½in wide white flowers appear over a long period from early summer to autumn. A range of other colours is available, including cream, pink and red, in single and double-flowered forms. H:1.2-1.5m/4-5ft; WT:7°C/45°F; W:☼; S:☼-○; cuttings, early to mid-summer; seeds, mid-summer.

1

2

STEPHANOTIS FAMILY **String of Hearts, Rosary Vine, Hearts Entangled** or **Heart Vine** *Ceropegia woodii* (**1**), from tropical Asia, Africa and Madagascar, is at its best when trailing from an indoor hanging-basket or a pot positioned at the edge of a high shelf. The thread-like stems often trail for 45cm/1½ft or more, bearing sparsely arranged, silvery marbled, heart-shaped leaves. It has also been called the Chinese Lantern because of the small, lantern-like, purple flowers. Good light and a relatively cool position are the secrets to success with this plant. Many plants in this family form large tubers and are used in salads. The stems and leaves are also eaten, while the tiny tubers that appear at the ends of some stems used as vegetables. Trailing; WT:7-10°C/45-50°F; W:☼; S:☼-○; division, summer; stem cuttings, early to mid summer; inserted at the ends of the stems, summer.

Shower of Stars or **Miniature Wax Flower** *Hoya bella* (**2**), from India, is one of the choicest of all scented climbers and trailers for the home. It is rather shrubby, with pendulous stems revealing 5cm/2in wide umbrella-like heads of star-shaped, waxy, white flowers from early summer to early autumn. The flower centres are shades of purple or red. It does well in a small pot, where the stems can trail, or in an indoor hanging-basket. Good light during winter is essential, so place it near to a window. H:23-30cm/9-12in; S:38-45cm/15-18in; WT:10-13°C/50-55°F. W:○; S:○-◑; cuttings, early to mid-summer.

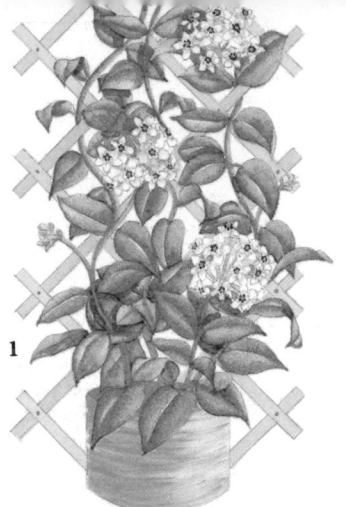

STEPHANOTIS FAMILY (contd) **Porcelain Flower** or
Wax Flower *Hoya carnosa* (**1**), from Queensland, is
vigorous and needs a large pot. It also needs a
supporting framework, and is ideal for growing up a
trellis near to a large window. From early summer to
early autumn it reveals 7.5cm/3in wide umbrellas of
fragrant, star-like flowers. H:1.8-4.5m/6-15ft; climber; WT:7-10°C/45-50°F; W:○; S:○-◉; cuttings,
mid-summer.

Orbea variegata (= *Stapelia variegata*) (**2**), from
Cape Province, is one of the Carrion Flowers, with

strongly marked, starfish-like and smooth-surfaced 7.5cm/3in wide flowers during mid to late summer. As implied by its common name, the flowers have very unpleasant carrion-like smells, which attract flies to pollinate them. The plant is found in areas where there are no bees, hence the flower's adaptation to fly pollination. It delights in full sun, and is ideal for sunny window-sills, even those in kitchens. H:10cm/4in; mat-forming; WT:5-10°C/41-50°F; W:☼; S:☼; seeds, early to mid-spring/division, early to late summer; cuttings, early to late summer.

Stapelia hirsuta (3) is another Carrion Flower from Cape Province with, as its name suggests, stems peppered with hairs. The 13cm/5in wide star-shaped flowers appear during mid to late summer, also covered by soft hairs that glisten and contrast with the yellow and brown petals. It grows rapidly and is one of the easiest stapelias to grow in the home, but it must have full sun. H:23cm/9in; clump-forming;

WT:5-10°C/41-50°F; W:☼; S:☼; seeds, early to mid-spring; division, early to late summer; cuttings, early to late summer.

STEPHANOTIS FAMILY (contd) **Madagascar Jasmine**
Stephanotis floribunda (**1**), from Madagascar, is also
called the Wax Flower, which leads to confusion with
Hoya carnosa. It is a vigorous climber when grown in
a conservatory or greenhouse, but it is adaptable
enough to be grown in a 15-20cm/6-8in wide pot in
the home. The heads of up to eight, 4cm/1½in long,
summer-to-autumn flowers are bathed in an exquisite
scent. It is best grown trained over a 45cm/2½ft high
hoop formed of pliable bamboo or split cane.
H:90cm-1.2m/3-4ft in a pot in the home; WT:10-
13°C/50-55°F; W:○; S:◉-●; cuttings, mid-spring to
mid-summer.

BEDSTRAW FAMILY **Coffee Plant** or **Arabian Coffee**
Coffea arabica (**2**), from the Ethiopian Highlands, is
mainly grown from seed and as a houseplant mainly
for the home. In Africa, it usually grows as a bush up
to 3m/10ft high. As a pot plant it is relatively
diminutive. It seldom produces its fragrant white
flowers in the home and is mainly grown for its
foliage. The best form for the home is 'Nana'. It was
in 1641 that England had its first opportunity to
sample the delights of coffee. Nathaniel Canopus, a
Cretan, made it his common beverage while at Balliol
College, Oxford. Its fame must have spread within
the confines of that city, for in Oxford in 1650 a Jew
called Jacobs opened the first coffee-house in
England.   H:60-75cm/2-2½ft;   S:38-45cm/15-18in;
WT:13°C/55°F;   W:○○;   S:○-◉;   seeds,   spring;
cuttings, summer.

BEDSTRAW FAMILY (contd) **Cape Jasmine** *Gardenia jasminoides* (**1**), from China, is a shrub with memorable, highly-fragrant, white and waxen flowers, 7.5cm/3in wide, mid to late summer. The winter-flowering form 'Veitchiana' is also superb, but needs a winter temperature of 16-18°C/61-64°F. As well as creating beautiful flowers, this genus yields plants with commercial applications. *G. lucida*, from India and Burma, produces a fragrant resin, while the fruit of another gardenia has been used to wash out stains in silk. H:0.6-1m/2-3½ft; S:60-90cm/2-3ft; WT:12°C/54°F; W:☼-○; S:○; cuttings, late winter to early summer.

2

VERBENA FAMILY **Bleeding Heart Vine** or **Glory Bower** *Clerodendrum thomsoniae* (**2**), from West Africa, is a tender, bushy, slow-growing evergreen climber, a member of a genus providing several hardy shrubs for the garden. This species creates early to late summer, lantern-shaped, white and deep crimson flowers in clusters up to 15cm/6in wide. It needs a framework up which it can climb and trail, near a window so that it gets the maximum possible light. H:2.4-3m/8-10ft in a pot in the home; climber; WT:13°C/55°F; W:○-◎; S:◎; cuttings, mid-spring to mid-summer.

LABIATE FAMILY **Flame Nettle** *Coleus blumei* (**3**), from Java, is well-known for its richly-coloured nettle-like leaves, although botanically it is not a member of the nettle family. The tubular, blue and white flowers appear during late summer and autumn, but are best nipped off so that they do not detract from the beauty of the leaves. It is a superb foliage plant for creating colour throughout summer, but avoid dull places as these reduce the brightness of the leaves. It is usually overwintered as cuttings taken in autumn. H:38-45cm/15-18in; S:30-38cm/12-15in; WT:13°C/55°F; W:☼-○; S:○; seeds, mid-winter; cuttings, early spring or late summer.

Candle Plant *Plectranthus coleoides* (**2**), from India, has a bushy habit. It is mainly grown for its foliage and is usually seen in the form 'Marginatus', with white and scalloped edges to the light green leaves. It grows up to about 30cm/1ft high, then it starts to cascade and trail, forming a superb plant for the edge of a shelf or an indoor hanging-basket. Keep the variegated form in good light. H:20-30cm/8-12in; S:20-30cm/8-12in; WT:7-10°C/45-50°F; W:☼-○; S:○; division, mid-spring to mid-summer.

Brazilian coleus *Plectranthus oertendahlii* (**1**), from South Africa, is an ideal prostrate foliage plant for indoor hanging-baskets or pots in wall-brackets, producing a cascade of 5cm/2in wide, rounded leaves. From early summer to autumn it displays 10-15cm/4-6in high candles of tubular flowers. H:15cm/6in;

spreading and trailing; WT:7-10°C/45-50°F; W:☼-◯; S:◯; division, mid-spring to mid-summer.

NIGHTSHADE FAMILY **Red Pepper, Green Pepper, Chilli** or **Winter Pepper** *Capsicum annuum* (**1**), from the tropics, is a short-lived perennial grown for its berries from summer to mid-winter. It is grown as an annual. The red, green or yellow fruits may be twisted, wrinkled, globular or cone-shaped. There are many varieties available. It is an ideal plant for brightening the home during winter, especially in a shady room. When introduced into Europe by the Spaniards and cultivated in England in 1548, it was known as Guinea Pepper or Pod-pepper. H:30-45cm/1-1½ft; S:30-38cm/12-15in; WT:7°C/45°F; W:☼; S:◐-●; seeds, early spring.

Poor Man's Orchid or **Butterfly Flower** *Schizanthus pinnatus* (**2**), from Chile, is one of the most spectacular flowering houseplants. During spring and early summer, it reveals masses of orchid-like, yellow, purple and rose flowers up to 4cm/1½in wide. Many dwarf forms are available, at 30-45cm/1-1½ft high, including 'Dwarf Bouquet', 'Monarch Mixed' and 'Hit Parade'. It is a good plant for brightening cool bedrooms and dining rooms. H:0.3-1m/1-3½ft; S:30-45cm/1-1½ft; WT:7°C/45°F; W:☼; S:○; seeds, late summer to early autumn.

Winter Cherry *Solanum capsicastrum* (**3**), from Brazil, is often confused with *Capsicum annuum*, which bears more elongated fruits. The Winter Cherry displays 12-18mm/½-¾in wide, marble-like and slightly

136

pointed fruits during winter, first yellow then bright red. The closely related Jerusalem Cherry, *S. pseudocapsicastrum*, with smaller fruits and smooth leaves, is often mistakenly sold as the Winter Cherry. The fruits of both these *solanums* should be regarded as poisonous and kept away from young children. H:30-45cm/1-1½ft; S:30-38cm/12-15in; WT:10°C/50°F; W:☼; S:☼; seeds, late winter to early spring.

1

2

NIGHTSHADE FAMILY (contd) *Streptosolen jamesonii* (**1**), from Colombia, is a tender, straggly, evergreen shrub, ideal in a large pot or tub. From late spring to mid-summer it bears lax, terminal, 10-20cm/4-8in long clusters of tubular, bright orange flowers. Secure shoots to canes or a framework against a wall. To prevent straggly growth, cut back old shoots by a third as soon as the flowers fade. H:1.2-1.8m/4-6ft; S:1.2-1.5m/4-5ft; WT:7°C/45°F; W:○; S:○-◐; cuttings, early to mid-spring.

FIGWORT FAMILY **Slipper Plant** *Calceolaria* x *herbeohybrida* (**2**) is gloriously decked with colour, from late spring to mid-summer, with 5-6.5cm/2-2½in long, pouch-shaped flowers in colours including yellow, orange and red, and variously spotted. It is one of the best early-flowering summer houseplants, and can also be flowered outdoors from mid to late summer in a sheltered position. There is a wide range of varieties, in various sizes, including dwarf types. Its symmetrical nature makes it ideal for brightening a dining table when not in use. Early botanists considered the flower to resemble a shoe, and the entire family were then named *Calceolarius* (Latin for shoemaker). H:23-45cm/9-18in; S:15-38cm/6-15in; WT:13°C/55°F; W:○; S:○-◐; seeds, mid-summer.

1

ACANTHUS FAMILY **Zebra Plant** *Aphelandra squarrosa* (**1**), from Brazil, has the most unforgettable leaves of all houseplants, with strikingly pale cream veining. The best form is 'Louisae'. From mid-summer to autumn, it is a further joy with terminal, cone-shaped, lantern-like spikes of rich yellow, tubular flowers. The North American common name, Saffron Spike, emphasises the eye-catching colour of these flowers. The plant can be admired best when it is grown on a low table, with a spotlight on it. After flowering, cut back the flowered shoots to a pair of healthy leaves. This encourages the development of new shoots that can be used to increase the plant. H : 30 - 60 cm / 1 - 2 ft ; S : 25 - 38 cm / 10 - 15 in ; WT:10°C/50°F; W:☼-○; S:○; cuttings, spring.

2

Firecracker Plant *Crossandra infundibuliformis (= C. undulifolia)* (P), from the East Indies, forms a compact, evergreen shrub, ideal in a pot. It can be grown in a conservatory, when it is grown on from season to season, but in the home plants are best discarded after the flowers fade, and fresh plants raised from seed in spring. From mid-spring to autumn it displays 2.5cm/1in wide, salmon-orange, flowers in spikes 10cm/4in long. After flowering, shorten all shoots by two-thirds on plants to be retained for another season. It is best grown as a floor-standing plant in a sunny position. H:60-90cm/2-3ft; S:45-60cm/1½-2ft; WT:13°C/55°F; W:☼; S:◎; cuttings, early spring to mid-summer; seeds, early spring.

ACANTHUS FAMILY (contd) **Shrimp Plant** *Justicia brandegeana (= Beloperone guttata)* (**1**), from Mexico is also known as the Mexican Shrimp Plant and False Hop. From spring to mid-winter it displays outstandingly beautiful, shrimp-like appendages up to 15cm/6in long. These are formed of colourful bracts and inconspicuous white flowers. Botanically, bracts are modified leaves. The Shrimp Plant retains its foliage throughout the year, and when it is in flower the compost must be kept moist. In late winter or early spring, lightly prune the plants. If cuttings are needed, remove them at this stage and root in 18°C/64°F. H:45-60cm/1½-2ft; S:30-45cm/1-1½ft; WT:7-13°C/45-55°F; W:○; S:◎-●; cuttings, early to mid-spring.

1

2

3

Fittonia verschaffeltii (**2**) from Peru, is a trailing evergreen houseplant for warm houses. Leaves have fine networks of carmine veins. Occasional, inconspicuous flowers are best nipped out when young. The best form is *F. v.* 'Argyroneura' (= *F. argyroneura*) with creamy-white veins and descriptively called the Lace-leaf Plant or Snakeskin Plant. In North America it has a wealth of names, including Mosaic Plant, Silver-net Plant, Nerve Plant, Silver Fittonia, and Silver-nerve. Position it where the stems are able to trail freely and reveal the very attractive leaves. H:trailing; WT:13-16°C/55-61°F; W:☼; S:◐-◉; division, mid-spring to late summer.

Polka Dot Plant *Hypoestes phyllostachya* (= *H. sanguinolenta*) (**3**), from Madagascar, is a spreading foliage houseplant that creates a wealth of subtly-coloured pink leaves. It can be easily raised from

143

seeds, although attractively coloured forms are best increased from cuttings to ensure new plants resemble the parent. It is useful as a pot plant in a wall bracket, or in an indoor hanging-basket. H:45-60cm/1½-2ft; S:45-60cm/1½-2ft; WT:10°C/50°F; W:○; S:◉; cuttings, spring; seeds, spring.

GLOXINIA FAMILY **Achimenes grandiflora** (**1**), from Mexico, is a bushy but upright deciduous perennial, well-known for its tubular, summer-long, five-petalled flowers that open flat, often to 5cm/2in wide. It is ideal for bringing indoors when in flower. In winter and until early spring, when the rhizomes are started into growth, it needs to be rested in a conservatory or cool place in the home. The achimenes group gained the name Hot Water Plants – it was wrongly thought that they needed watering with warm water, and this perpetuated the common name. H:45-60cm/1½-2ft; S:38-45cm/15-18in; WT:16°C/61°F during spring when the tubers are started into growth; W:○; S:◉; young tubers, early spring.

Achimenes heterophylla (**2**), from Guatemala, is smaller than the previous species, with similarly shaped flowers but only 4cm/1½in wide. The form 'Little Beauty' is bushier, with crimson-pink flowers. H:25-30cm/10-12in; S:20-25cm/8-10in; WT:16°C/61°F during spring when the tubers are started into growth; W:○; S:◉; young tubers, early spring.

Achimenes longifolia (**3**), from Central America, is about the same height as *A. heterophylla*, but with stems that splay out. The tubular flowers open to 5cm/2in wide, in colours from red to purple-blue. Several forms are available, including 'Major' violet-blue and 'Alba' white. H:30-38cm/12-15in; S:45-60cm/18-24in; WT:16°C/61°F during spring when the tubers are started into growth; W:○; S:◎; young tubers, early spring.

1

2

3

GLOXINIA FAMILY (contd) **Basket Vine** or **Lipstick Vine** *Aeschynanthus radicans* (= *A. pulcher/Trichosporum lobbianum*) (**1**), from Java, is an outstanding evergreen plant for an indoor hanging-basket, where the 90cm/3ft long stems can trail freely. During early to mid-summer they bear many 4.5cm/1½in long, hooded, flowers along their tips. In its native habitat the plant trails from the tops of jungle trees, and it is therefore essential that it is positioned where stems can trail. H:45-60cm/1½-2ft; S:45-60cm/1½-2ft and trailing; WT:7-13°C/45-55°F; W:☼; S:☼-○; cuttings, early to mid-summer.

Aeschynanthus speciosus (= *Trichosporum speciosum*) (**2**), from Indonesia, is a superb summer-flowering evergreen plant for an indoor hanging-basket. The tubular and clustered, 5-6.5cm/2-2½in long, bright orange flowers create a blaze of colour which is especially effective when seen at eye-height. Established plants need re-potting every third or fourth year. H:20-60cm/8-24in; S:30-45cm/12-18in; WT:7-13°C/45-55°F; W:☼; S:☼-◐; cuttings, early to mid-summer.

Columnea x *banksii* (**3**) is less trailing than the two following columneas. However, the 60-90cm/2-3ft long, pendulous stems bear larger flowers, 6.5-7.5cm/2½-3in long, from early winter to mid-spring. It is an ideal plant for an indoor hanging-basket. Trailing; WT:13-16°C/55-61°F; W:○; S:◐-●; cuttings, early spring to early summer.

GLOXINIA FAMILY (contd) *Columnea gloriosa* (**1**), from Costa Rica, is an especially beautiful trailing and flowering plant, ideal for an indoor hanging-basket or a position that enables the 0.75-1.2m/2½-4ft long stems to trail unimpeded. The 5-6.5cm/2-2½in long, bright scarlet, hooded flowers clothe the stems from autumn to spring, and are superb for bringing winter colour to the home. Trailing; WT:13-16°C/55-61°F; W:○; S:◎-◉; cuttings, early spring to early summer.

Columnea microphylla (**2**), again from Costa Rica, is small leaved and ideal for a hanging-basket secured high enough for the 1.2-1.8m/4-6ft long stems to trail. The hooded, 4-5cm/1½-2in long, bright orange-scarlet flowers appear from early winter to mid-spring. Well-grown and mature plants present an unforgettable winter display. All *columneas* are known as Goldfish Plants. Trailing; WT:13-16°C/55-61°F; W:○; S:◉-●; cuttings, early spring to early summer.

Flame Violet *Episcia cupreata* (**3**), from tropical America, is superb where the stems are able to trail. Plant it in an indoor hanging-basket, or in a pot positioned at the edge of a shelf. Alternatively, stand the container on an inverted flower pot. The stems bear bright silver-and-green, soft and furry, leaves. During early summer it bears small, red flowers. Ensure moisture does not fall on the leaves. H:30-38cm/9-15in, S:30-38cm/12-15in, trailing and spreading; WT:18-21°C/64-70°F; W:☼-○; S:○-◉; division, summer; cuttings, spring.

Clog Plant or **Pouch Flower** *Hypocyrta glabra* (**4**), from South America, gains its common names from the orange-red, tubular, flowers borne in summer. The fleshy, evergreen, glossy-green foliage forms an ideal foil for the flowers, as well as providing year-through interest. After the flowers fade, pinch back the stems by about 10cm/4in to encourage fresh shoots and bushiness. H:15-20cm/6-8in; S:20-30cm/8-12in; WT:15°C/59°F; W:○; S:◉; cuttings, spring.

GLOXINIA FAMILY (contd) **African Violet** *Saintpaulia ionantha* (**2**), from the coastal area of Tanzania, has a wide range of flower colours and a neat, rounded shape. Flowering is usually from early summer to autumn, although it can be throughout the year. There are many named varieties, mostly in single colours, but some bicolored, in single, semi-double and double forms. H:7.5-13cm/3-5in; S:15-23cm/6-9in; WT:13°C/55°F; W:○; S:◎; cuttings, mid to late summer; seeds, early to mid-spring.

Gloxinia *Sinningia speciosa* (= *Gloxinia speciosa*) (**3**), a tuberous-rooted plant from Brazil, known for its velvety leaves and bell-shaped 5-10cm/2-4in long flowers chiefly from early summer to early autumn. Named varieties are available in white, red, pink and purple. H:23-25cm/9-10in; S:23-30cm/9-12in; WT:21°C/70°F for starting tubers into growth in late winter; W:○; S:◎; seeds, late winter to early spring; division, early spring; leaf-cuttings, mid-summer.

Temple Bells *Smithiantha hybrids* (**1**) have been created from a number of crosses between several species, resulting in plants with a wealth of flower colour including pink, red, yellow, orange, yellow and white. These foxglove-like flowers are revealed in large, pyramidal heads, and appear from early to late summer. H:45-60cm/1½-2ft; S:30-45cm/1-1½ft; WT:21°C/70°F for starting the tubers into growth in late winter or early spring; W:☼; S:○-◎; division of tubers, late winter to early summer; leaf-cuttings, early to mid-summer.

151

1

2

GLOXINIA FAMILY (contd) **Cape Primrose** *Strepto-carpus* x *hybridus* (**2**) is another beautiful hybrid plant, with foxglove-like, 4-6.5cm/1½-2½in long flowers, borne in small clusters from early summer to autumn. Colours include white, red and purple, with the best known named form being 'Constant Nymph', displaying satiny, bluish-purple flowers. H:23-30cm/9-12in; S:23-38cm/9-15in; WT:10°C/50°F; W:○; S:○-◐; seeds, early to mid-spring for plants to flower the following year; leaf-cuttings, early to mid-summer.

BELLFLOWER FAMILY **Italian Bellflower** or **Star of Italy** *Campanula isophylla* (**1**), from Northern Italy, is an ideal trailing perennial plant for an indoor hanging-basket in a porch, hallway or cool room. During mid-summer to autumn, it displays a wealth of star-shaped, 2.5cm/1in wide, blue flowers that smother the leaves. A white-flowered form is available, as well as 'Mayii', with variegated leaves. H:10-13cm/4-5in; S:30-45cm/1-1½ft and trailing; WT:2°C/35°F; W:◐; S:◐; division, spring; cuttings, mid to late spring.

DAISY FAMILY **Chrysanthemums** *Chrysanthemum* (**3**), whose origins can be traced back to China and Japan, are widely sold throughout the year as flowering pot plants. They are grown by specialist nurserymen, who control the periods of light and dark given to them to ensure flowering plants are available throughout the year. Once the plants have finished flowering, they are best discarded and fresh ones bought. Chemicals are often used to dwarf vigorous varieties, and such plants never bloom the following year in any satisfactory manner, if at all. There are many varieties and colours available. These are superb as table-centre decorations and in cool bedrooms. H:20-38cm/8-15in; S:20-30cm/8-12in; WT:2°C/35°F; W:○-◉; S:○-◉; buy fresh plants as houseplants.

Gynura aurantiaca (**1**), from Java, is grown for its sprawling and climbing nature, with stems and leaves covered with bright, violet-purple hairs. During late winter, it develops clusters of orange flowers, slightly resembling those of Groundsel, but they do not have a pleasant smell. Take care that water does not splash on the leaves, which can be soon damaged during summer if bright light falls on moisture-covered leaves. Its sprawling natures makes it ideal for planting where the stems can freely trail. H:60-90cm/2-3ft; S:38-45cm/15-18in; WT:10-13°C/50-55°F; W:○; S:◉-◉; cuttings, mid-spring.

Velvet Plant or **Purple Passion Vine** *Gynura procumbens* (= *G. sarmentosa*) (**2**), from India, is a climber or trailer, ideal in an indoor hanging-basket or pot where it can sprawl. It is grown for its leaves that are covered with fine purplish hairs. During spring, it bears 12mm/½in long, orange flowers in terminal clusters. Like the previous plant, the flowers are not pleasantly scented. H:1.2-1.5m/4-5ft when climbing; WT:10-13°C/50-55°F; W:○; S:◉-◉; cuttings, mid-spring.

DAISY FAMILY (contd) **Cineraria** *Senecio cruentus* (= *Cineraria cruenta*) (**3**), from the Canary Islands, is a wonderful houseplant for creating colour from mid-winter to early or mid-summer. Plants are best bought when in bud, with colour just showing. The large leaves become smothered with daisy-like, 18-50mm/¾-2in wide, flowers held in large heads. Many varieties are available, in colours including pink, red, lavender, blue, mauve and white, as well as in bicolors. Ensure the compost does not dry out when the plants are in flower. Its symmetrical outline makes it an ideal plant for brightening a dining table, when not in use, or a cool bedroom. H:30-45cm/1-1½ft; S:25-38cm/10-15in; WT:8-10°C/46-50°F; W:○; S:○-◉; seeds, spring to mid-summer.

String-of-beads *Senecio rowleyanus* (**1**), from South-west Africa, is a trailing succulent, best grown in an indoor hanging-basket or pot positioned on a high shelf, where the long, slender stems display their grape-like leaves which resemble beads. From late summer to early winter, the sweetly-scented, white flowers, with purple stigmas, appear sparsely on 5cm/2in long stems. H:5cm/2in; S:60-90cm/2-3ft long trailing stems; WT:7-10°C/45-50°F; W:○; S:○-◉; stem-cuttings, mid-summer; division, early to late summer.

LILY FAMILY ***Aloe aristata*** (**2**), from Cape Province, eventually produces a large clump of rosettes. The stemless rosettes are formed of narrow leaves, up to

10cm/4in long, and covered with slightly raised, white spots. If plants become too large, rosettes can be removed and rooted. Highly attractive flowers appear during early summer, on long, thin stems up to 38cm/15in high. H:10-15cm/4-6in; S:10-13cm/4-5in; WT:5°C/41°F; W:☼; S:○-◉; offsets, summer; seeds, early spring.

LILY FAMILY (contd) **Partridge-breasted Aloe** *Aloe variegata* (**1**), from Cape Province, is a well-known succulent, ideal for sunny window-sills. The keel-shaped, 13cm/5in long, leaves are attractively marked with white bands. An added feature are the tubular, orange flowers on stems 25-30cm/10-12in high during late spring. H:20-25cm/8-10in; S:13-15cm/5-6in; WT:5°C/41°F; W:☼; S:○-◉; offsets, summer; seeds, early spring.

Asparagus densiflorus '**Sprengeri**' (= *A. sprengeri*) (**2**), from Natal, South Africa and known in North America as the Emerald Fern and Emerald Feather, is ideal in hanging containers, where its green foliage on wiry stems create year-round interest. The form 'Compactus' is a dwarf variety, more erect and less trailing and best grown in pots. Take care not to give it high temperatures, especially during winter. In summer it is superb for decorating cool, shady rooms. H:25-30cm/10-12in; S:75-90cm/2½-3ft; WT:41-

45°C/5-7°C; W:○; S:◎-◉; division, early to mid-spring/seeds, mid-spring.

Asparagus Fern *Asparagus setaceus (= A. plumosus/ Asparagopsis setacea)* (**3**), from South Africa, is also known as the Lace Fern. Despite its common names, it is not a fern but a member of the lily family. Eventually, it reaches 3m/10ft high, but is seldom seen other than in its smaller and more manageable form, when it makes an excellent foliage pot plant with feathery needle-like green foliage. It is the fern frequently used by florists as a backing for wedding button-holes. The best type for growing in pots is 'Compactus', a dwarf and non-climbing form. H:60-75cm/2-2½ft in juvenile form; S:30-60cm/1-2ft in juvenile form; WT:5-7°C/41-45°F; W:○; S:◎-◉; division, early to mid-spring; seeds, mid-spring.

3

LILY FAMILY (contd) **Cast Iron Plant** or **Parlour Palm** *Aspidistra elatior* (**2**) is well known in North America as Bar-room Plant. This reflects the tolerant nature of this Chinese plant, so long associated with handle-bar moustaches, bustles, gas-lights, musical evenings and parlours. Its hey-day was at the turn of the century, but it is still well worth growing, especially the variegated form, with green leaves striped whitish-cream. Unfortunately, this variegated form is not so tolerant of neglect as its all green brother, and requires more light. H:30-38cm/12-

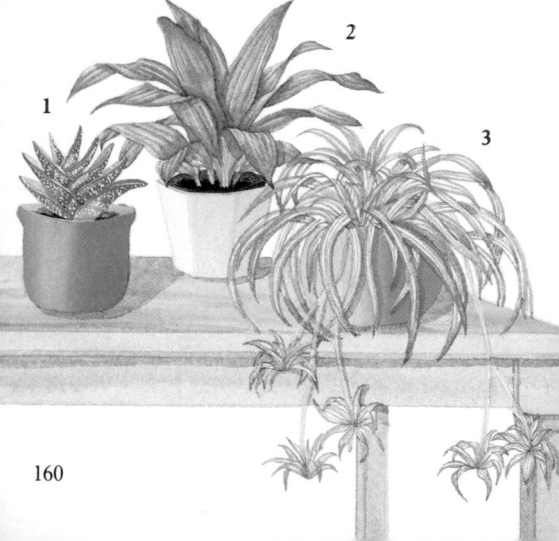

15in; S:45-60cm/18-24in; WT:7-10°C/45-50°F; W:○;
S:◉-●; division, early to mid-spring.

Spider Plant or **St. Bernard's Lily** *Chlorophytum capense* (= *C. elatum*) (**3**) is a widely grown South African houseplant, well noted for its long, narrow, pale to mid-green leaves. It is often confused with *C. comosum* (= *C. sternbergianum*) which is grown mainly for its variegated forms. These include 'Variegatum' with green leaves edged white and 'Vittatum' with a central white strip and green edges. An interesting aspect of this species is the stiff but arching stems that bear plantlets at their ends. When pegged into compost, they readily produce roots. These plants have roots that swell and tend to push the complete soil-ball out of the pot. This often prevents the roots being thoroughly watered and suggests that the plant has reached a stage when it needs repotting H.20-25cm/8-10in, S.38-60cm/15-24in; WT:7°C/45°F; W:○; S:○-◉; division, early to mid-spring; plantlets, summer.

Gasteria maculata (**1**), from South Africa, creates an attractive and widely grown plant with strap-shaped and flattened, 15cm/6in long and 4cm/1½in wide, leaves. In young plants these tend to form two rows, rather than a rosette, and soon produce offsets that rapidly expand the plant's width. It is very resilient and well suited to offices, as well as homes. H:15-20cm/6-8in; S:15-23cm/6-9in or more; WT:5°C/41°F; W:☼; S:○-◉; seeds, spring; division, summer.

LILY FAMILY (contd) *Haworthia margaritifera* (**1**), from South Africa, is a widely grown succulent. The leaves, created in a slender rosette, are attractively peppered with pearly tubercles. During mid-summer, it develops small, bell-like flowers on wiry stems. It is ideal for a window-sill in the home or in offices. H:7.5-10cm/3-4in; S:13-15cm/5-6in; WT:5°C/41°F; W:☼-◉; S:☼-◉; offsets, mid-summer; seeds, spring.

Haworthia maughanii (**2**), from South Africa, is a diminutive, slow-growing, choice succulent with semi-cylindrical leaves arranged in rosettes. They appear to have had their tops sliced off. In their native desert conditions the plants are almost buried, with just the transparent 'windows' at their tops exposed to light. However, when grown in the home, the leaves are left completely above the compost. This helps to prevent rotting if the compost is kept too wet. During early autumn it bears small, bell-like, white flowers. H:2.5cm/1in; S:7.5-13cm/3-5in; WT:5°C/41°F; W:☼-◉; S:☼-◉; seeds, spring.

Common Hyacinth *Hyacinthus orientalis* (**3**), from Western Asia and Eastern Europe, is a spectacular bulb for the home. The highly scented, candle-like, 10-15cm/4-6in high spires can be flowered indoors from mid-winter to late spring. Specially prepared bulbs can be potted in autumn and given cool conditions to encourage the development of roots and shoots. Later, they are brought into gentle heat. A wide range of varieties is available, in white, cream, cerise-pink, red, lilac-mauve, blue and purplish-blue. Take care not to place the flowering bulbs in a high temperature. H:15-23cm/6-9in; S:10-13cm/4-5in; WT:10°C/50°F when in flower; W:☼; S:○; buy fresh bulbs each year for forcing.

3

LILY FAMILY (contd) **Tulips** *Tulipa* (**1**) make colourful splashes of colour when forced into flower indoors from mid-winter to spring. The best types for forcing into flower in the home are the early dwarf varieties, which rise to about 30cm/1ft, and are available in a wide colour range. Do not attempt to grow the large, tall types indoors. During autumn, plant three or five bulbs in well-drained compost or bulb fibre in a 15cm/6in wide pot. They then need a cool, dark place for the development of roots and shoots. Inspect the pots every 14 days to ensure the compost does not dry out. When the leaves are 2.5-5cm/1-2in above the compost, move the pots to a cool room, with a temperature about 10°C/50°F, until the shoots are 10cm/4in high. The temperature can then be raised to 18°C/64°F. After flowering, move the pots to a cool, frost-proof corner, and in early summer plant the bulbs under shrubs. The bulbs cannot be forced into flower the following year. H:30cm/1ft - dwarf and early types; WT:see text; use fresh bulbs each year.

Forest Lily *Veltheimia viridifolia (= V. undulata)* (**2**), a bulbous plant from South Africa, is a delight from late winter to late spring, with pink, tubular flowers on strong stems. After flowering, the plant dies down and the bulb needs resting. In early autumn repot the bulb, leaving it half exposed. H:38-50cm/15-20in; S:20-25cm/8-10in; WT:10°C/50°F; W:☼-○; S:○; offset bulbs, early autumn.

165

1

AGAVE FAMILY **Century Plant** or **American Aloe**
Agave americana 'Marginata' (**1**), from Mexico, is
hardy enough to be placed outside on a sheltered
patio during summer. When young, it makes a
superb plant for the home. The spine-tipped,
yellow-edged, stiff and thick, green leaves form a
rosette. Eventually, the plant will flower, although
this is rare with plants in pots indoors. Flowering can
be both a well-discussed joy and total disaster, for
after blooming the whole plant dies. This must be the
perverse face of Mother Nature! However, the name
Century Plant originated to indicate the plant's
longevity before falling prey to its doomsday
reproduction technique. The tissue of this plant has
been widely used in the production of ropes and for
the feeding of cattle, while with some species the juice
of the leaves has been used as a substitute for soap. A
gallon of the juice yields about a pound of soft soap.
H:75-90cm/2½-3ft; S:0.75-1m/2½-3½ft; WT:5°C/
41°F; W:☼; S:☼-○; offsets, summer.

Thread Agave *Agave filifera* (**2**), from Mexico,
displays leathery, stiff and tapering leaves about
2.5cm/1in wide, beautifully marked with white,
thread-like lines along their edges. It blooms when
between eight and twenty years old, throwing up a
stem to 2.4m/8ft and bearing large, bell-like, purple
and green flowers. The main rosette then dies, but
others develop around its base. H:38-45/15-18in;
S:45-6-cm/1½-2ft; WT:5°C/41°F; W:☼; S:☼-○;
offsets, summer; seeds, spring.

1

AGAVE FAMILY (contd) *Agave parviflora* (**1**) is a
beautiful diminutive agave from Mexico, forming a
neat rosette with stiff, miniature, dagger-like, white-
edged leaves with white threads along the edges.
Eventually, it produces a 1m/3½ft high flower stem,
and then dies. Fortunately, young plantlets form
around the dying rosette. Try it on a bright
window-sill. H:20cm/8in; S:18-20cm/7-8in; WT:5°C/
41°F; W:☼: S:☼-○; offsets, summer; seeds, spring.

168

Agave victoriae-reginae (**2**), from Mexico, is ideal in
the home, greenhouse or conservatory, although it is
not as hardy as other agaves. It forms a neat,
symmetrical, rosette with stiff and keeled leaves. It is
superb on a large window-sill. H:20-25cm/8-10in;
S:38-50cm/15-20in; WT:5°C/41°F; W:☼; S:☼-○;
seeds, spring.

AGAVE FAMILY (contd) **Cabbage Palm** *Cordyline australis* (*= Dracaena australis*) (**3**) comes, as its name suggests, from Australia and New Zealand, where it forms a cabbage-headed tree up to 7.5m/25ft high. However, when grown in the restricted compost area in a 15-20cm/6-8in pot in the home it is slow growing, to only 90cm/3ft high. It can be placed outside on sheltered patios during warm summers. Eventually it is ideal as a floor-standing plant near a patio window. H:75-90cm/2½-3ft; S:30-38cm/12-15in; WT:4-7°C/39-45°F; W:○; S:○-◉; suckers, early to mid-spring; cuttings, early to mid-summer; seeds, spring.

Ti Plant, Ti Log or **Flaming Dragon** *Cordyline fruticosa* (*= C. terminalis*) (**2**), from tropical Asia, is often erroneously called *Dracaena terminalis*, a species to which it is related. It gains its name Flaming Dragon from the green leaves that are variegated with flame-red flashings. Eventually, the plant forms a stem, and in tropical countries is often cut up and sold to tourists as Ti Logs. These can be inserted into compost, and eventually root and form a new plant. Several named forms are available, including 'Guilfoylei', with red and pink or white striped leaves, and 'Tricolor', where they are red and purple. H:45-90cm/1½-3ft; S:38-45cm/15-18in; WT:10-13°C/50-55°F; W:○; S:○-◉; suckers, early to mid-spring; cuttings, early to mid-summer; seeds, spring.

Cordyline indivisa (*= Dracaena indivisa*) (**1**) comes from New Zealand, where it rises to 6m/20ft and is called Toii or Broad-leaved Cabbage Tree. In a pot in the home, however, it can be contained to a manageable size, with an unbranched single stem. It is ideal as a floor-standing plant, set at the back of a group of low-growing plants, over which its leaves can hang. H:0.9-1.2m/3-4ft; S:45-60cm/1½-2ft; WT:4-7°C/39-45°F; W:○; S:○-◉; suckers, early to mid-spring; cuttings, early to mid-summer; seeds, spring.

AGAVE FAMILY (contd) ***Dracaena deremensis*** (**1**), evergreen and eventually tree-like from tropical Africa, is a colourful foliage plant for the home. The sword-like leaves, up to 45cm/1½ft long, display interesting stripes. 'Bausei' reveals dark green leaves with white centres, 'Rhoersii' (**1**) has a pale green central stripe, edged with fine white bands, and 'Warneckii' with dark green borders and a distinctive white stripe. H:1-1.5m/3½-5ft; S:38-45cm/15-18in; WT:13°C/55°F W:○; S:○-◉; cuttings, early to mid-spring.

Ribbon Plant *Dracaena fragrans*, from West Africa and Guinea, bears a resemblance to *D. deremensis*, but has a wider spread, with strap-like leaves up to 90cm/3ft wide. Two forms are popular: 'Massangeana', often called the Corn Plant, with golden-centred and green-edged leaves, and 'Lindenii' (**4**), displaying broad, gold edges and narrow gold centres. H:1.2-1.5m/4-5ft; S:60-75cm/2-2½ft; WT:13°C/55°F; W:○; S:○-◉; cuttings, early to mid-spring.

Dracaena godseffiana (**2**), from the Congo, is unlike most other *dracaenas*. It forms a branching evergreen shrub with wiry stems bearing cream-spotted green leaves up to 7.5cm/3in long. H:60-90cm/2-3ft; S:38-45cm/15-18in; WT:10°C/50°F; W:○; S:○-◉; cuttings, early to mid-spring.

Dracaena sanderiana (**3**), from the Congo, is initially well suited to the home, where it forms an eye-catching foliage houseplant in a small pot. If given a large pot, about 25cm/10in wide, it eventually reaches 2.1m/7ft. H:45-60cm/1½-2ft in a small pot; S:38-45cm/15-18in; WT:10°C/50°F; W:○; S:○-◉; cuttings, early to mid-spring.

AGAVE FAMILY **Mother-in-Law's Tongue** or **Snake Plant** *Sansevieria trifasciata* 'Laurentii' (**2**), from West Africa, is widely seen in homes where it forms an attractive foliage plant. In North America it is also known as Devil's Tongue. The shorter form, 'Hahnii' (= *S. hahnii*), rises to 15cm/6in, with curved and triangular, stiff, dark green leaves with transverse bands of yellow. All *sansevierias* are known as Bowstring Hemp, their fibres being used as bowstrings in Central Africa and Asia. H:38-45cm/15-18in; S:15-20cm/6-8in; WT:7-10°C/45-50°F; W:☼; S:☼-◉; suckers, summer.

Yucca aloifolia (**1**), from Mexico, southern North America and the West Indies, is a tender relative of the yuccas that grace our gardens, and is widely grown in pots indoors where it creates a distinctive plant. In North America it is known as Spanish Bayonet or Dagger Plant, and these aptly describe the stiff leaves. Another tender yucca frequently sold is the Spineless Yucca *Y. elephantipes* (= *Y. guatemalensis*). *Y. brevifolia*, from North America, is widely known as the Joshua Tree. It often reaches 12m/40ft and at one time forests of it skirted the Southern Pacific Railway through the Mohave Desert. The fibrous, 30cm/1ft thick, stems proved excellent for conversion into paper, and it has been used to make newsprint. H:1.2-1.5m/4-5ft; S:30-45cm/1-1½ft; WT:7-10°C/45-50°F; W:☼; S:☼-○; stem-cuttings, mid-spring to mid-summer.

1

2

175

DAFFODIL FAMILY ***Clivia miniata*** (**2**), from Natal, is a superb bulbous plant for the home or conservatory. The strap-like, wide-spreading leaves splay outwards, and from spring to late summer reveal a stout stem

bearing upright clusters of orange to red flowers. Pot up fresh bulbs singly in spring. It is superb as a decoration for dining tables when not in use. H:38-45cm/15-18in; S:38-45cm/15-18in; WT:16°C/61°F for planting in spring; W:☼-○; S:○-◉; division of bulbs, late winter to early spring.

Haemanthus katherinae (**3**), from Natal, is a tender bulbous plant, best grown in a large pot, 15-20cm/6-8in wide. During summer it bears oustandingly attractive, 15cm/5in wide, flower heads. The bulbs are large and best planted during early spring, with their necks just covered. Repot them every three years. H:30cm/1ft; S:30-38cm/12-15in; WT:10°C/50°F; then 16°C/61°F in the growing season; W:☼-○; S:☼ ○; offsets, spring.

Hippeastrum Hybrids (**1**), known in North America as Amaryllis or Barbados Lily, are well-known bulbous plants for the home. The *hippeastrum* species, from which these hybrids are derived, originally came from South America. Hippeastrums are less hardy than their near relatives Amaryllis, but by potting up bulbs periodically throughout the year a succession of flowers can be produced. Three or four flowers are borne at the tops of one or two stiff, upright stems. Plant only one bulb in each pot, with half exposed. A wide colour range is available, including pink, red, white and orange. H:30-45cm/1-1½ft; S:15-23cm/6-9in; WT:13-16°C/55-61°F; W:○; S:○; seeds, early spring, but mixed results from hybrids.

DAFFODIL FAMILY (contd) **Daffoldils** *Narcissus* (**1**) are superb in the garden in spring and can be just as welcome in the home when forced into flower to create colour from mid to late winter. Specially-prepared bulbs are the best types to buy, planting them in pots of bulb fibre - or a mixture of loam, peat and sand - from late summer to late autumn. Set the bulbs close together, with their noses just above the compost. They need cool conditions for about 8-12 weeks, until shoots are 10-13cm/4-5in high and the roots well developed. Then, slowly increase the temperature from 7°C/45°F to 15°C/60°F. H:25-38cm/10-15in; S:close together in a pot; WT:see above; W:○-◎; bulbils, but fresh bulbs are best used for forcing each year. Bulbs, after they have flowered, can be planted around shrubs in the garden.

Scarborough Lily *Vallota speciosa* (= *V. purpurea*) (**2**), from South Africa, is a brightly-coloured bulbous plant, flowering indoors from mid-summer to early autumn. Plant fresh bulbs in pots in late summer, leaving their tops exposed. Set one bulb to each pot. Keep the compost moist, but not waterlogged. It is an ideal plant for a cool room during summer, and looks good when positioned in an unused fireplace in a bedroom. This plant is said to have gained its common name from a Dutch ship with a cargo of these bulbs that was wrecked close to Scarborough, in Yorkshire, but it may just be that the flower was well known in that area through its importation through the port which gained bonding status in 1841.

H:45-60cm/1½-2ft; S:20-30cm/8-12in; WT:5-7°C/
41-45°F; W:☼; S:☼-○; offsets, early autumn.

1

2

BROMELIAD FAMILY **Amazonian Zebra Plant** or **Queen of the Bromeliads** *Aechmea chantinii* (= *Billbergia chantinii*) (**3**), from Peru and Brazil, is a spectacular bromeliad with a funnel-shaped rosette of stiff leaves, colourfully banded. During late summer and autumn, it bears stunningly attractive yellow to red flowers on stiffly erect stems. As with all aechmeas, keep the central funnel filled with water. Also, they all grow well in lime-free, open-textured compost. H:60-75cm/2-2½ft; S:30-38cm/12-15in; WT:13-16°C/55-61°F; W:○-◉; S:○-◉; removal of rooted shoots from the base of the plant, when about one-third the size of the parent plant.

Urn Plant, Exotic Brush, Silver Vase or **Vase Plant** *Aechmea fasciata* (= *Billbergia rhodocyanea*) (**2**), from Brazil, is perhaps the best known bromeliad, widely grown for its 15cm/6in long flower heads borne from mid-summer through to winter. First they are blue, later rose-pink. It is one of the easiest bromeliads to grow. Keep the central vase full of water. H:45-60cm/1½-2ft; S:38-45cm/15-18in; WT:13-16°C/55-61°F; W:○ ◉; S,○-◉; removal of rooted shoots from the base of the plant, when about one-third the size of the parent plant.

Aechmea fulgens (**1**), from Brazil, is one of the smaller aechmeas and ideal for the home, where it is widely used to decorate both dining and coffee tables. The broad green leaves form a rosette, from which develops waxen-blue flowers during late summer and early autumn. An interesting form with purple undersides to the leaves is *A. f. discolor*. H:30-38cm/12-15in; S:30-38cm/12-15in; WT:13-16°C/55-61°F; W:○-◉; S:○-◉; removal of rooted shoots from the base of the plant, when about one-third the size of the parent plant.

1

2

BROMELIAD FAMILY (contd) **Pineapple** *Ananas comosus* (= *A. sativus*) (**2**), from Brazil and Colombia, is a well known succulent fruit, first taken to Europe in about 1661 and named after a pine cone, which the fruit resembles. In was 1715 before the first edible pineapple was grown in Britain, by Sir Mathew Decker in his garden at Richmond, London. For the development of edible fruits, a consistently high temperature is needed, about 26°C/80°F, although dense heads of purplish flowers are often produced by plants in the home. Therefore, it is best grown for its decorative qualities. H:60-90cm/2-3ft; S:45-60cm/1½-2ft; WT:18°C/65°F; W:☼; S:☼-O; removal of rooted shoots from the base of the plant, early to mid-spring.

Red Pineapple *Ananas sapenaria* (= *A. bracteatus*) (**1**), from Brazil, is similar to *A. comosus*, but with showier flower heads. An attractive form is 'Striatus', with eye-catching, narrow and sword-like, green leaves with creamy-white edges. Set on a wide window-sill, it forms a superb, eye-catching plant. H:45-75cm/1½-2½ft; S:45-60cm/1½-2ft; WT:18°C/65°F; W:☼; S:☼-O; removal of rooted shoots from the base of the plant, early to mid-spring.

BROMELIAD FAMILY (contd) **Angel's Tears** or **Queen's Tears** *Billbergia nutans* (**1**), from South America, is one of the most spectacular bromeliads, with 7.5-10cm/3-4in long, drooping, clusters of 2.5-4cm/1-1½in long flowers borne on arching stems. It creates a superb display when allowed to arch and spread; do not position other plants too close to it. A brightly lit, round, dining room table creates a good setting for it. H:38-45cm/15-18in; S:38-45cm/15-18in; WT:16-18°C/61-64°F; W:○; S:○-◎; removal of rooted shoots from the base of the plant, when half the size of the parent plant.

Summer Torch *Billbergia pyramidalis* (= *B. thyrsoidea*) (**2**), from Brazil, bears short-lived but repeated,

1

184

10-15cm/4-6in long spires, formed of orange-pink bracts and blue and red flowers, during mid-summer. H:30-38cm/12-15in; S:25-30cm/10-12in; WT:16-18°C/61-64°F; W:○; S:○-◑; removal of rooted shoots from the base of the plant, when half the size of the parent plant.

Billbergia x 'Windii' (**3**) has *B. nutans* in its parentage, but reveals a more foliage-packed and slightly compacter form. Clustered heads of 2.5-4cm/1-1½in long tubular flowers appear during summer. Its semi-pendulous shape is best not intruded upon by other plants, as it spoils the plant's character. H:38-45cm/15-18in; S:38-45cm/15-18in; WT:16-18°C/61-64°F; W:○; S:○-◑; removal of rooted shoots from the base of the plant, when half the size of the parent plant.

BROMELIAD FAMILY (contd) ***Cryptanthus acaulis*** *(= C. undulatus)* (**1**), from Brazil, is a delightful bromeliad for the home, or even in a bottle garden where its slow growth makes it an ideal candidate for a restricted area. It is grown for its rosette of wavy-edged and spined leaves. Forms available include 'Rubra' with purple-brown shading over-laying green, and the pretty 'Argenteus' (**2**) with silver-scaled leaves. All *cryptanthus* plants are commonly known as Starfish Plants or Earth Stars. H:6.5-7.5cm/2½-3in; S:10-13cm/4-5in; WT:16-18°C/61-64°F; W:☼-◐; S:☼-◐; offshoots, spring.

Cryptanthus bivittatus (**3**), from Brazil, is another rosette-forming bromeliad, zoned in light and dark green. It does not have such a symmetrical outline as *C. acaulis*, with one or two leaves much longer than the others. It is ideal for a window-sill in a bright, warm kitchen, or in a bottle garden. However, do not position the bottle garden in full sun, as the glass may act as a lens and burn the leaves. H:7.5-9cm/3-3½in; S:20-30cm/8-12in; WT:16-18°C/61-64°F; W:☼-◐; S:☼-◐; offshoots, spring.

Cryptanthus zonatus (**4**), from Brazil, is a low-growing bromeliad, forming a wide, rosette-like star. The leaves, as the botanical name suggests, are attractively banded. Like other cryptanthus plants, it adores good light, and grows well on window-sills. H:9-10cm/3½-4in; S:15-23cm/6-9in; WT:16-18°C/61-64°F; W:☼-◐; S:☼-◐; offshoots, spring.

1

1

3

4

187

BROMELIAD FAMILY (contd) ***Guzmania monostachys***
(= *G. tricolor*) (**1**), from the West Indies, Brazil and
Florida, is an evergreen bromeliad, suited to the
home as well as for growing in a conservatory. It is the
long-lasting, cylindrical, 38cm/15in long flower spike
for which the plant is chiefly grown. It grows well on
a low table away from direct light. Like all
guzmanias, it is best watered with rain water, and
given acid soil. H:38-45cm/15-18in; S:20-30cm/8-
12in; WT:16-18°C/61-64°F; W:; S:◉-; offshoots,
spring.

Guzmania sanguinea (**3**), from Colombia, forms a
beautiful rosette of wide, strap-shaped leaves that
curve outwards and downwards. The 6.5cm/2½in
long, yellow or white, tubular, three-petalled flowers
are short-lived. It looks at its best when seen from

above, so place it on a coffee table - and highlight it with a table lamp. H:20-30cm/8-12in; S:20-25cm/8-10in; WT:16-18°C/61-64°F; W:◎; S:◎-◉; offshoots, spring.

Blushing Bromeliad *Neoregelia carolinae (= Nidularium meyendorffii)* (2) is a superb bromeliad from Brazil, with stiff, strap-like, bright green leaves that form a central vase about 5cm/2in wide. When in flower - and this may be at any time of the year - the central vase of leaves becomes bright red and appears to blush, as suggested by the common name. The flower spike rises from the urn, revealing violet-blue flowers. The form 'Tricolor' is widely grown, producing leaves longitudinally striped ivory-white. Good light helps to bring out the full colour of the leaves. H:30cm/1ft; S:30-40cm/12-15in; WT:18°C/65-61°F; W:◎; S:◎ ◉; offshoots, mid-summer.

3

BROMELIAD FAMILY (contd.)***Nidularium fulgens*** (=
N. pictum/Guzmania picta) (**1**), from Brazil, shares the
same common name as some other bromeliads. The
wide, strap-like and speckled leaves arch to form a
rosette from which a 7.5cm/3in wide head, formed of
2.5-5cm/1-2in wide bracts and three-petalled tubular
flowers, appears. H:25-30cm/10-12in; S:25-38cm/10-
15in; WT:15-18°C/59-64°F; W:☼-○; S:○-◉; offshoots, mid-summer.

Tillandsia lindenii (= *T. lindeniana*) (**2**) is a
bromeliad from Peru, with long, narrow leaves
displaying purple undersides. During summer it
reveals a 15-20cm/6-8in long, lantern-like, flattened
spike on a 30cm/1ft stem. It needs high humidity – so
syringe it frequently with rain water or boiled, cooled
tap water. Every three to four weeks, add a weak,
liquid fertilizer to the water. As well as being planted
in a pot holding equal parts leaf-mould, peat, sand
and sphagnum moss, it can be grown by removing
offsets and gluing them on to pieces of driftwood or
gnarled bark. A related South American species, *T.
usneoides*, is known as Tree-beard. It yields a mass of
black fibres which were used for stuffing cushions.
H:38-50cm/15-20in; S:30-38cm/12-15in; WT:13°C/
55°F; W:○; S:○-◉; offshoots, mid-summer.

BROMELIAD FAMILY (contd) **Vriesea fenestralis** (**1**), from Brazil, does not have the immediate leaf colour impact of the two following species, but it is a plant that catches the eye - throughout the entire year. The broad, strap-shaped leaves are longitudinally striped with dark green veins. During summer, it reveals a 45cm/1½ft high spike of 6.5cm/2½in long, tubular flowers.   H:60-75cm/2-2½ft;   S:38-45cm/15-18in; WT:18-21°C/64-70°F;   W:○;   S:○-◑;   removal of rooted shoots from the base of the plant, when half the size of the parent plant.

King of Bromeliads or **Bromeliad King** *Vriesea hieroglyphica* (**2**), from Brazil, derives its botanical name from the dark and irregular markings on the broad, strap-like leaves that form a rosette. During spring it develops a 60-75cm/2-2½ft high stem, topped with 5cm/2in long flowers. It is ideal for decorating a dining table, when not in use, or a coffee table. H:60cm/2ft; S:38-45cm/15-18in; WT:18-21°F/64-70°; W:○; S:○-◉; removal of rooted shoots from the base of the plant, when half the size of the parent.

Flaming Sword *Vriesia splendens* (**3**), from Guyana, forms a rosette with beautiful, cross-banded, sword-like leaves that seldom fail to attract. It gains its common name from the late summer spike, burgeoned with colour from the 5-7.5cm/2-3in long flowers and bracts. It needs a high temperature and frequent syringing with rain water. H:50-60cm/20-24in; S:38-50cm/15-18in; WT:18-21°C/64-70°F; W:○; S:○-◉; removal of rooted shoots from the base of the plant, when half the size of the parent plant.

SPIDERWORT FAMILY *Callisia elegans* (= *Setcreasea striata*) (**2**), from northern Mexico, is known in North America as the Striped Inch Plant, because of its white striped leaves and close relationship to tradescantias. The undersides of the leaves are a beautiful reddish-purple. The plant will sprawl or climb, but is at its best when trailing from the edge of a shelf. Alternatively, plant it in an indoor hanging-basket. Trailing; WT:7°C/45°C; W:○-◎; S:◎-◕; cuttings, spring.

Boat Lily or **Moses in a Cradle** *Rhoeo spathacea* (= *R. discolor*) (**3**), an evergreen foliage plant from Mexico and the West Indies, needs a high spring temperature and high humidity. Frequent syringing with rain water is essential, especially during summer. When young, it forms a rosette of lance-shaped leaves up to 20cm/8in long, but with maturity develops a short stem. The leaves have purplish undersides.'Vittatum' (often sold as 'Variegata), has leaves finely striped with cream. H:25-30cm/10-12in; S:20-30cm/8-12in; WT:7-10°C/45-50°F (16°C/61°F in spring); W:◎; S:◎-◕; cuttings, mid-spring; seeds, mid to late spring,.

Setcreasea pallida **'Purple Heart'** (= *S. purpurea*) (**1**), from Mexico, is an extremely tolerant foliage plant for the home, well able to withstand neglect. It is mainly grown for the tufted, 15cm/6in long, narrow and lance-shaped, purple leaves. Good, but not strong, sunlight is the key to attractive leaf colour. From early summer to winter it bears purple bracts

that surround the 12-18mm/½-¾in wide, rose-purple flowers. These are borne on stems up to 30cm/1ft high. Its sprawling nature suits an indoor hanging-basket or the edge of a shelf. H:30-38cm/12-15in; S:38-45cm/15-18in; WT:7°C/45°F; W:○; S:○-◎; cuttings, early to late summer.

195

SPIDERWORT FAMILY (contd) **Wandering Jew**
Tradescantia albiflora (= *T. viridus*) (**1**), from South
Africa, is mat-forming and trailing, ideal for an
indoor hanging-basket or wall-mounted pot. It is also
a good shelf plant. Invariably, it is offered for sale in
a variegated form, such as 'Tricolor', with rose-
purple and white stripes. Trailing; WT:7-10°C/45-
50°F; W:○; S:◐-●; cuttings, late spring to late
summer.

Flowering Inch Plant or **Inch Plant** *Tradescantia
blossfeldiana* (**2**), from Argentina, is excellent for any
position where it can trail. It bears purple stems,
displaying stiff leaves, longer than those in most
tradescantias. From early spring to mid-summer it
reveals 12-18mm/½-¾in wide, white-centred, rose-
purple flowers. Trailing; WT:7-10°C/45-50°F; W:○;
S:◐-●; cuttings, late spring to late summer.

Trandescantia fluminensis (= *T. myritifolia*) (**3**),
from South America, is similar to *T. albiflora*, but
with shorter leaf stalks and slightly longer leaves. It
is easy to grow, and available in a range of
coloured-leaved forms. The best one is 'Quicksilver',
with silver-striped leaves. Plants that become leggy
with bare centres can easily be replaced by taking
cuttings which root within several weeks. Trailing;
WT:7-10°C/45-50°F; W:○; S:◐-●; cuttings, late
spring to late summer.

SPIDERWORT FAMILY (contd) *Zebrina pendula* (**1**) is a superb trailing foliage plant from Mexico, often confused with tradescantias. Indeed, in North America it is known as the Inch Plant. The stiff stems bear leaves with a lustrous, crystalline texture above, and suffused purple below. It also has the charm of 12mm/½in wide, three-petalled, purple flowers from early summer to autumn. The form 'Quadricolor' displays white and purple striping on the upper surfaces. Trailing; WT:7-10°C/45-50°F; W:○; S:◑-◉; cuttings, early to late summer.

Bronze Inch Plant *Zebrina purpusii* (= *Tradescantia purpurea*) (**2**), again from Mexico, is best positioned where its leaves - larger than those of *Z. pendula* - can trail. Its terminal clusters of rose-purple flowers appear in late autumn, and closely resemble those of *Z. pendula*. Trailing; WT:7-10°C/45-50°F; W:○; S:◑-◉; cuttings, early to late summer.

PALM FAMILY **Parlour Palm** *Chamaedorea elegans* (= *Neanthe bella/Collinia elegans*) (**3**), from Mexico and Guatamala, is a delightful palm, often sold when 15-20cm/6-8in high, in small collections of house-plants for table-top decoration. Usually, the other plants mature and die, leaving the palm which can then be grown on its own for many years. It has been grown as a houseplant since well before the turn of the last century, when it became known as the Parlour Palm. In North America it is known as the Good Luck Palm. In Central America it is used, together with several other species, to form walking sticks, while the unexpanded flower spikes are used by Mexicans as a vegetable called Tepejilote. H:0.75-1.2m/2½-4ft;　　S:0.75-1m/2½-3½ft; WT:12°C/54°F; W:○; S:◎-◑; seeds, spring.

1

2

3

PALM FAMILY (contd) **European Fan Palm** *Chamae-rops humilis* (**1**), from the western Mediterranean, Malta and southern Portugal, is a beautiful palm. In the wild it creates a large clump, sometimes 4.5m/15ft high and with sucker-like growths. In the home it is less adventuresome and well suited to filling a large corner. In warm areas it is hardy enough to survive on a sheltered patio during summer. At one time the leaves were widely used in southern Europe for making hats, brooms and baskets, as well as for house thatching. The coarse hair from around the bases of the leaves was used by Arabs for mixing with camel's hair to create tent covers. H:1.5-2.4m/5-8ft; S:0.90-1.5m/3-5ft; WT:4°C/40°F; W:○; W:◐-◉; suckers, summer.

Areca Palm or **Butterfly Palm** *Chrysalidocarpus lutescens* (= *Areca lutescens*) (**2**) from Madagascar has a fine and feathery nature and before they are fully open the leaves appear skeletonized. Eventually it grows up to 6m/20ft high and 2.1m/7ft wide but when young is superb for the home. The related *Areca catechu*, from Asia, produces Betal Nuts - also known as Areca Nuts or Pinang - that resemble nutmegs. They are cut into narrow pieces and rolled up with a little lime in the leaves of the Betel Pepper, *Chavica betle*. Apart from the saliva that stained teeth, it also produced intoxication and is so addictive that some Madagascars would rather forgo meat and drink than their favourite areca nuts. Perhaps as some sort of compensation for the leaves discolouring teeth, the nuts can be roasted and the charcoal used to clean teeth. H:1.2-2.4m/4-8ft; S:0.9-1.5m/3-5ft; WT:15°C/59°F; W:○; S:◐-◉; seeds, spring.

PALM FAMILY (contd) **Sentry Palm** *Howeia belmoreana (= Kentia belmoreana)* (**1**), from the Pacific Lord Howe Islands, suggests for many people the foyers of grand hotels in the Twenties and Thirties. It is best seen in an alcove or corner with a white background, where the green fronds are highlighted. Its large and graceful fronds, up to 30cm/1ft wide and 45cm/1½ft long, create a dominant feature. It gains its old botanical name, *Kentia*, from the main town on the Lord Howe Islands, which are about 400 miles off the eastern coast of Australia. In North America it is well known as the Belmore Sentry Palm and the Curly Palm. H:1.8-3m/6-10ft; S:1.5-2.4m/5-8ft; WT:10-12°C/50-54°F; W:☼; S:○-◐; seeds, late winter.

Kentia Palm *Howeia forsteriana (= Kentia forsteriana)* (**2**), from the Pacific Lord Howe Islands, is known in North America as the Thatch Palm and Sentry Palm, and these superbly describe the stance and radiating nature of the leaves, up to 45cm/1½ft long and 30cm/1ft wide. It looks distinguished when two are positioned either side of an entrance, especially against a white background. It also looks good in an alcove. H:1.8-3m/6-10ft; S:1.5-2.4m/5-8ft; WT:10-12°C/50-55°F; W:☼; S:○-◐; seeds, late winter.

Microcoelum weddelianum (= Cocos weddeliana/Syagrus weddeliana) (**3**), from South America, is one of the prettiest and most delicate of all small palms. It is slow growing and ideal for positioning on a Victorian plant stand or a small side-table. It is usually seen at not more than 30cm/1ft high, but can become larger. H:1.8m/6ft; S:1.2-1.5m/4-5ft; WT:16°C/61°F; W:☼; S:○-◎; seeds, late winter to early spring.

1

2

3

1

2

PALM FAMILY (contd) **Canary Island Date Palm**
Phoenix canariensis (**2**), from the Canary Islands, is a
superb palm for the home, and hardy enough to be
placed outside on a warm patio during summer.
Indoors, in a large pot - or small tub in a conservatory
- it creates a dominant feature, and is especially
attractive when positioned by the side of a large patio
window. Flowers are seldom produced on young
plants, and rarely on plants indoors. H:1.2-1.8m/4-
6ft; S:0.9-1.5m/3-5ft; WT:7°C/45°F; W:☼; S:○-◎;
seeds, late winter to early spring.

Date Palm *Phoenix dactylifera* (**1**), from North Africa,
is the palm that produces the commercial dates. In its
native country it rises to 18-24m/60-80ft, but in a pot
in the home will be manageable until it is 10 or 15
years old. In North Africa it often lives to over
one-hundred years and without doubt is a versatile
plant - rather like the pig, nothing is wasted. Apart
from the fruits, it produces a wine called Lagbi, the
hearts of the young leaves have been used as a
vegetable, the leaf-stalks employed in the construc-
tion of baskets and wicker-work, while the fibres
surrounding the leaf-stalks are used in rope manufacture. H:3-4.5m/10-15ft; S:2.4-4.5m/8-12ft;
WT:10°C/50°; W:☼; S:○-◎; seeds, late winter to
early spring.

205

PALM FAMILY (contd) **California Fan Palm** *Washingtonia filifera* (**1**) is a fast-growing palm from California, Colorado and Arizona, where it often reaches 24.5m/80ft. In the home, it creates a rapid-growing but short-lived pot plant, with large fronds of brilliant green leaves with reddish stems. Unfortunately, as the plant matures segments of the leaves drop off. Like *W. robusta*, it has fine, cotton-like, threads hanging between the leaf segments, which gained both the name American Cotton Palms. It has also been called the Desert Fan Palm. If it becomes too large for the home, it can stand outside on a warm and sheltered patio during

summer.   H:1.8-3m/6-10ft;   S:1.2-1.5m/4-5ft;
WT:7°C/45°F; W:☼; S:☼-◐; seeds, early spring.

Mexican Fan Palm *Washingtonia robusta* (**2**) is a
fast-growing palm from Mexico, where it is called the
Thread Palm or Mexican Washington Palm and is
grown as a street tree. There, it becomes bare around
its base, with the thatch of leaves falling, and often
reaches 24.5-30m/80-100ft. In the home, however, it
creates an attractive pot plant that can be put out on
a warm and sheltered patio during summer. H:1.8-
3m/6-10ft; S:1.2-1.5m/4-5ft; WT:7°C/45°F; W:☼;
S:☼-◐; seeds, early spring.

ARUM FAMILY *Aglaonema commutatum* (**3**), from Malaya and the Philippines, is grown for its decorative, lance-shaped, silvery-green marked evergreen foliage. During mid-summer, it develops 5cm/2in long, arum-like, white flower heads, followed by attractive dark red berries. Warmth and humidity are essential for good growth. Create extra humidity by standing your plant in a water-filled saucer of pebbles. H:15-20cm/6-8in; S:23-30cm/9-12in; WT:10-16°C/50-61°F; W:○; S:◎; basal shoots and suckers, mid to late spring; seeds, spring.

Aglaonema pictum (**2**), from Sumatra and Malaya, displays beautifully stippled leaves and 5cm/2in long, arum-like, yellow-green flowers from mid to late summer. Although aglaonemas like a certain amount of root restriction, do not forget to feed them every two to three weeks during summer with a weak, liquid fertilizer. H:15cm/6in; S:23cm/9in; WT:16-18°C/61-65°F; W:○; S:◎; basal shoots and suckers, mid to late spring; seeds, spring.

Aglaonema treubii (**4**), from Indonesia, is a superb plant for the home, and similar to *A. commutatum*. Its lance-shaped leaves radiate from stiff stems at the plant's centre, forming a good plant for a low table where the foliage can be admired from above. H:23cm/9in; S:30cm/12in, WT:10-16°C/50-61°F; W:○; S:◎; basal shoots and suckers, mid to late spring; seeds, spring.

Painter's Palette, Wax Flower or **Oil-cloth Flower** *Anthurium andreanum* (**1**), from Colombia, is spectacular. Its heart-shaped and palette-like, waxy red or white, 10cm/4in long and 7.5cm/3in wide, spathes are borne from early summer to early autumn. Although not always symmetrical, it makes an unusual and attractive plant for table-centre decoration during summer. Water your plant generously, and syringe it with rain-water to create a humid atmosphere. H:38-45cm/15-18in; S:30-38cm/12-15in; WT:13-16°C/55-61°F; W:◎; S:◎; division, early to mid-spring; seeds, spring.

ARUM FAMILY (contd) ***Anthurium crystallinum*** (**2**), from Colombia, is best known for its velvety, 60cm/2ft long and 30cm/1ft wide, heart-shaped leaves. Eventually, the leaves mature to reveal ivory veins on a deep green background. The late spring to early autumn flowers are inconsequential. It is best positioned on a low table or on the floor where it cannot be damaged – the leaves are best seen from above. H:38-45cm/15-18in; S:30-38cm/12-15in; WT:13-16°C/55-61°F; W:◎; S:◉; division, early to mid-spring; seeds, spring.

Flaming Flower, Pigtail Flower or **Tail Flower** *Anthurium scherzerianum* (**1**), from Guatemala, is smaller than its two brother species and bears elongated, 18cm/7in long, arrow-shaped leaves and waxy-textured, bright red, 7.5-10cm/3-4in long, spathes that hang on stiff, wiry stems from spring to late autumn. The common names derive from the spathes which have curled, orange-red, wick-like appendages at their centres. H:20-25cm/8-10in; S:30-45cm/12-18in; WT:10-13°C/50-55°F; W:◎; S:◎; division, early to mid-spring.

Angel's Wings *Caladium* x *hortulanum* (**3**) is tuberous-rooted and grown for its large, handsome, spear-shaped leaves in a wide colour range, as well as combinations of shades. Specific forms include 'Candidum', with a network of green veins, 'Pink Cloud', mottled pink, 'Seagull', with beautiful broad white veins, and 'Stoplight', suffused crimson with narrow, green edges. Beware of placing your plant in a gloomy position, as this prevents the attractive colours in the leaves from appearing. H:23-38cm/9-15in; S:25-30cm/10-12in; WT:21°C/70°F for starting the tubers in early spring; W:◎; S:◎-◉; offsets, early spring.

ARUM FAMILY **Leopard Lily** or **Dumb Cane**
Dieffenbachia maculata (= D. picta) (**1**) is a strikingly
attractive foliage plant from Brazil and Colombia,
bearing oblong, variably coloured leaves up to
30cm/1ft long. Named forms include 'Bausei', with
leaves in shades of green and with silver spots,
'Exotica', suffused yellow and green, and 'Roehrsii',
pale yellow with some veins in ivory. It is a very
adaptable plant, being equally attractive in a group of
other houseplants as when in a white, porcelain pot

1   2

and positioned as a decoration for a table. The common name Dumb Cane is highly descriptive of the plant. All parts are poisonous, especially the sap. If it gets into the mouth, speech is prevented for some time. It is said that in the West Indies cruel planters made stubborn, vociferous and unmanageable slaves eat pieces of the plant. However, in the reign of King Charles II a physician recommended the juice of the plant to be administered internally as a cure for dropsy! Nevertheless, it is wise to keep this attractive plant away from the prying hands of children, and the teeth of family pets. H:0.45-1m/1½-3½ft; S:25-45cm/10-18in; WT:13-16°C/55-61°F; W:☼; S:○-◉; cuttings, mid-spring to mid-summer.

Swiss Cheese Plant *Monstera deliciosa* (= *Philo dendron pertusum*) (**2**), from Mexico, is one of the most popular foliage plants for the home, but eventually needs plenty of space if it is to be seen at its best. The leaves in mature plants can be 1m/3½ft long and 45-60cm/1½-2ft wide. Initially, they are slit at their sides, slowly forming elongated holes or deep notches. The name *deliciosa* refers to the delicious fruits. Mature plants develop large, creamy-yellow, arum-like flowers with parts that develop into green, elongated, pineapple-like fruits. They are said to have a luscious pineapple and banana flavour. Unfortunately, these seldom appear on plants grown in the home. H:1.8-3.5m/6-12ft; S:0.75-1.5m/2½-5ft; WT:7-10°C/45-50°F; W:☼; S:○-◉; cuttings, mid-summer.

ARUM FAMILY (contd) **Tree Philodendron** *Philodendron bipinnatifidum (= P. lundii)* (**2**), from Brazil, does not have a nature that confirms its common name - it is a non-climbing species. Initially, the leaves are heart-shaped and without indentations, but after a couple of years, as the plant matures, they become deeply incised and three-lobed. Eventually, they may be 60cm/2ft long and 45cm/1½ft wide. It is an ideal plant for filling a large corner area. H:1-1.2m/3½-4ft; S:0.9-1m/3-3½ft; WT:13-16°C/55-61°F; W:○; S:○-◉; seeds, mid-spring; division, early to mid-summer, but first removing the growing tips a year earlier.

Elephant's Ear or **Spade-leaf Philodendron** *Philodendron domesticum (= P. hastatum)* (**3**), from Brazil, is a climber with glossy, spear-shaped leaves up to 18cm/7in long. For added attraction, try the variegated form, with leaves marked in cream and yellow. H:1.2-1.8m/4-6ft; S:23-38cm/9-15in; WT:13-16°C/55-61°F; W:○; S:○-◉; cuttings, early to mid-summer.

Blushing Philodendron *Philodendron erubescens* (**1**) from Colombia is a climber that reveals the accuracy of its common name. When they emerge the 23cm/9in long arrowhead-shaped leaves are rose-pink, later becoming a beautiful copper-tinged dark glossy green. The best form is 'Burgundy' with copper-red young foliage. H:1.2-1.8m/4-6ft; S:30-45cm/1-1½ft; WT:13-16°C/55-61°F; W:○; S:○-◉; cuttings, early to mid-summer.

ARUM FAMILY **Philodendron melanochryson** (= *P. andreanum*) (**1**), known in North America as Black-gold Philodendron, is a climber from Colombia. In its juvenile form, 1.2-1.8m/4-5ft high, it displays velvety, dark green leaves, 15cm/6in long, elongated and heart-shaped. The adult, arrow-shaped leaves, up to 60cm/2ft long, are seldom seen on plants in the home. It is at its best when trained up a moss-covered pole, which also helps to provide a damp surface for the aerial roots to cling to and to absorb additional moisture. Position the plant in a corner of the room, preferably against a light-coloured background. H:1.2-1.8m/4-6ft; S:30-45cm/1-1½ft; WT:13-16°C/55-61°F; W:○; S:○-◎; cuttings, early to mid-spring.

Sweetheart Vine *Philodendron scandens* (**3**) is a climber from Panama and probably the most widely grown philodendron in homes. It can be planted in a small pot, 7.5cm/3in wide, when it will grow only a foot or so high, or in a large pot and trained to climb a trellis several feet high. It can also be grown as a trailing plant - nip out the growing tips several times to encourage bushiness. Like other climbing philo-dendrons, it is especially attractive when climbing a moss-covered pole. H:0.60-1.5m/2-5ft when climbing; WT:13-16°C/55-61°F; W:○; S:○-◎; cuttings, early to mid-spring.

Peace Lily or **Sail Plant** *Spathiphyllum wallisii* (**2**) is an evergreen perennial from Colombia and best known for its late spring to mid-summer arum-like white flowers that stand slightly above the shiny lance-shaped leaves. It is similar to anthuriums, but more tolerant and easier to grow. The hybrid *S.* 'Mauna Loa' displays slightly larger and brighter flowers. Take care not to let the compost become dry, as the foliage will then shrivel and wilt. H:23-30cm/9-12in; S:30-38cm/12-15in; WT:10-13°C/50-55°C; W:☼; S:○-◎; division, mid-spring.

1

2

ARUM FAMILY (contd) **Arrowhead Vine** or **Goose-foot Plant** *Syngonium podophyllum* (2), from Mexico and Panama, is an attractive climber, although it will also trail. In young plants the leaves are arrow-shaped, with lobes resembling rabbit's ears. In maturity they become trifoliate and display several lobes, the central one up to 30cm/1ft long. Mature plants also develop arum-like flowers, sometimes followed by fruits, but this is rare in pot-grown plants. Variegated forms are available, such as 'Green Gold' and 'Imperial White'. It develops aerial roots and when grown as a climber it is best given a moss-covered pole to climb. H:0.6-1.2m/2-4ft; S:38-45cm/15-18in; WT:13°C/55°F; W:◉; S:◉-◉; stem cuttings with roots attached, spring to mid-summer.

SCREW PINE FAMILY **Screw Pine** *Pandanus veitchii* (1), from Polynesia, is grown for its long, narrow, spiny-edged and colourfully striped leaves that spread and splay outwards. Old specimens often develop stems, but usually the plant is seen as a large rosette of leaves. The common name refers to the cork-screwed stems of mature plants. It is best grown as a specimen plant, rather than mixed in with other houseplants, so that the beautiful leaves can be clearly seen. A related Screw Pine, *P. utilis*, from Madagas-car, was commonly planted alongside sugar-fields and the processed leaves used for thatching and for making sugar sacks and high-class Manila hats. H:45-60cm/1½-2ft; S:45-60cm/1½-2ft; WT:10-13°C/50-55°F; W:☼; S:○-◉; offshoots, spring.

SEDGE FAMILY **Umbrella Grass, Umbrella Plant** or **Umbrella Palm** *Cyperus alternifolius* (**2**), from Africa, delights in moisture and can be grown in water to a depth of 15cm/6in, but in the home it thrives in a pot placed in a shallow saucer of water. The common names aptly describe the leaves, which radiate like the spokes of an umbrella from the tops of stiff stems. It is ideal for growing in a small group of other houseplants, where they all help to create a more humid atmosphere than if placed separately around a room. The form 'Variegatus' creates extra interest, with its white striped leaves and stems. *C. diffusus* is another frequently grown species, and slightly taller. The roots of several cyperus plants have been used as food. *C. esculentus*, known in North America as Nut Grass, has been used in southern Europe as a food. The tuberous roots, when roasted and ground, have been used as substitutes for coffee and cocoa. H:60-75cm/2-2½ft; S: 45-60cm/1½-2ft; WT:13°C/55°F; W:○; S:○-◉; division, spring to late summer; seeds, early spring to early summer.

BANANA FAMILY **Bird of Paradise Flower** *Strelitzia reginae* (**1**), also known as Crane Flower and Crane Lily, is from South Africa, and unforgettable with its mid-spring, bird-like heads held on stiff, upright stems. Eventually, it needs a conservatory or greenhouse, but even as a small plant it seldom fails to attract interest with its spectacular flowers. It belongs to the banana family and was named in honour of Princess Charlotte of Mecklenburg-Strelitz

(1744-1818), later Queen to George III of England. Each spring, many of these flowers are flown into Britain from the Madeira Islands to decorate rooms. H:0.9-1.2m/3-4ft; S:0.9-1.5m/3-5ft; WT:10°C/50°F; W:☼; S:☼-○; division, early summer⁷; seeds, early to mid-spring.

ARROWROOT FAMILY **Rattlesnake Plant** *Calathea lancifolia (= C. insignis)* (**4**), from Brazil, is a distinctive and elegant foliage plant, with upright, lance-shaped and snakeskin-like leaves. It forms an attractive plant for a side-table, especially when illuminated by a table-lamp to highlight the colourful leaves. H:20-25cm/8-10in; S:20-23cm/8-9in; WT:13-16°C/55-61°F; W:○; S:◉-●; division, mid-summer.

Peacock Plant *Calathea makoyana* (**3**), from Brazil, is a particularly showy house plant. The 15cm/6in long, oblong leaves appear painted in many colours, and when seen against a light are extremely beautiful. H:38-45cm/15-18in; S:30-45cm/12-18in; WT:13-16°C/55-61°F; W:○; S:◉-●; division, mid-summer.

Calathea ornata (**1**), from Colombia and Equador, is often seen in the home, but can be variable. The 18cm/7in long, dark green, thin and papery leaves usually display pinkish veining, changing to cream. Like all other calatheas, it is superb when positioned on a coffee table, so that the leaves can be closely admired. H:38-45cm/15-18in; S:38-45cm/15-18in; WT:13-16°C/55-61°F; W:○; S:◉-●; division, mid-summer.

Zebra Plant *Calathea zebrina* (**2**), from Brazil, reflects its common name by revealing contrasting, light and dark green banding on the leaves. For complete success it needs warmth and a very humid position. Mist spray the foliage several times a day, and position out of draughts. H:38-45cm/15-18in; S:38-

45cm/15-18in; WT:13-16°C/55-61°F; W:○; S:◎-◉;
division, mid-summer.

Never Never Plant *Ctenanthe oppenheimiana* 'Tricolor' (**5**), from Brazil, is a superb foliage plant, with elongated, spear-shaped leaves bodly banded in constrasting colours, often tinted cream, with purple undersides. It is ideal for positioning in a group of houseplants, where its somewhat sprawling nature helps to unify the arrangement. H:20-30cm/8-12in; S:25-38cm/10-15in; WT:16°C/61°F; W:○; S:○-◎; division, late spring to early summer.

ARROWROOT FAMILY (contd) **Domino Plant** or
Rabbit Track Plant *Maranta leuconeura massangeana*
(**1**), from Brazil, is also known as the Prayer Plant,
because the leaves close together in the evening and
are held erect. The 10cm/4in long leaves are
beautifully blotched, and with ivory veins. It is
superb either in a group of other houseplants or as a

specimen on a polished dining room table. A form of arrowroot, a nutrious starch, is derived from the roots of *M. arundinacea*, also known as the Bermuda or West Indian Arrowroot. H:15-20cm/6-8in; S:20-30cm/8-12in; WT:10-13°C/50-55°F; W:◐; S:◐-●; division, mid-spring; cuttings, early to late summer.

Maranta leuconeura erythroneura (= *M. l. tricolor*) (**2**), from Brazil, is also known as the Prayer Plant. The 15cm/6in long leaves are slightly longer than in the previous plant, and often more erect. Also, it is less easy to grow, being intolerant of chills. Place it on tables, away from draughty windows and doors. H:15-23cm/6-9in; S:20-30cm/8-12in; WT:10-13°C/50-55°F; W:○; S:◐-●; division, mid-spring; cuttings, early to late summer.

ORCHID FAMILY **Cœrnes. Flower** *Cattleya bowringiana* (**4**), from Guatemala, is easy to grow and flower. From late summer to mid-winter, it develops stems with up to ten, 7.5cm/3in wide, rose-purple flowers. H:45-60cm/1½-2ft; S:15-20cm/6-8in; WT:11-13°C/52-55°F; W:○-◐; S:◐; division, late spring to early summer.

Coelogyne cristata (**3**), from the Himalayas, is ideal for the home. From mid-winter to mid-spring it bears pendulous, 15cm/6in long, spikes of 5-7.5cm/2-3in wide, fragrant, white flowers. It flowers best when growing in a root-congested pot. H:50cm/20in; S:30-38cm/12-15in; WT:10°C/50°F; W:○-◐; S:◐; division, early spring to early summer.

ORCHID FAMILY (contd) *Cymbidium* Hybrids (**1**) develop 7.5-13cm/3-5in wide flowers from autumn to mid-summer. Many named forms are available, in a wide colour range. These include Angelica 'Advent' (13cm/5in wide yellow flowers from autumn to winter); Ayres Rock 'Cooksbridge Velvet' (11cm/4½in wide crimson tinged with white, and rich dark crimson lips during winter and spring); Dingwall 'Lewes' (13cm/5cm wide white flowers during late spring); Fort George 'Lewes' (12.5cm/4¾in wide green flowers during winter and spring); Peter Pan 'Greensleeves' (7.5cm/3in wide soft green flowers during autumn); Stonehaven 'Cooksbridge' (7cm/2¾in wide pale yellow and dark edged flowers during autumn and winter); and Touchstone 'Janis' (2.5-4cm/1-1½in wide bronze flowers with contrasting deep crimson lips during winter and spring. H:45-75cm/1½-2½ft; S:38-45cm/15-18in; WT:10°/50°F; W:○; S:◎; division, early spring to early summer.

3

Dendrobium densiflorum (?), from the Himalayas. Is an easily-grown orchid, with beautiful pendulous bunches of 5cm/2in wide, golden-yellow flowers from early spring to early summer. The flower heads often display 50 to 100 blooms. H:30-38cm/15-18in; S:30cm/1ft; WT:10°C/50°F; W:○-◉; S:◉-◉; division, early spring.

Dendrobium 'Gatton Sunray' (3) is a spectacular hybrid with arching stems of bright red and yellow, 10cm/4in wide, flowers during summer. It needs tying to a supporting cane, which both secures the stems and shows the flowers to perfection. H:1.2-1.5m/4-5ft; S:60-90cm/2-3ft; WT:13°C/55°F; W:○-◉; S:◉-◉; division, early spring.

ORCHID FAMILY **Cinnamon Orchid** *Lycaste aromatica* (**2**), from Mexico, is well known for its sweetly-scented, 5cm/2in wide, yellow flowers during winter and early spring. Only one flower is borne on each stem, but a mature plant may produce as many as thirty flowers. H:30-38cm/12-15in; S:20-30cm/8-12in; WT:10-13°C/50-55°F; W:○-◎; S:◉; division, early spring to early summer.

Oncidium ornithorhynchum (**3**), from Mexico and Guatemala, is easy to grow and flower. From autumn to mid-winter it displays sweetly-scented, 2.5cm/1in wide, lilac-pink flowers on long, arching stems. It grows well on a window-sill in the home. H:60cm/2ft; S:38-45cm/15-18in; WT:10°C/50°F; W:○; S:◎-◉; division, early to mid-spring.

Lady's Slipper Orchid, Slipper Orchid or **Venus' Slipper** *Paphiopedilum* 'Maudiae' (**1**) is well-known and easy to grow and flower. It is a cross between two green-flowered orchids, and during summer develops a white flower with delicate green shading. H:45cm/1½ft; S:20-25cm/8-10in; WT:13°C/55°F; W:○-◎; S:◉; division, late winter to early summer.

Pleione formosana (**4**), from Tibet to Formosa, is widely and easily grown, with mid-winter to early spring, 7.5-10cm wide flowers on 15cm/6in high stems. The flowers colour ranges from pure white to pale pink-mauve. It is an ideal orchid for indoors. H:15-20cm/6-8in; S:15-20cm/6-8in; WT:4°C/39°F; W:○-◎; S:◉; offsets, mid to late spring.

3

4

2

Index

230

234